Salmon House

on the Hill Cookbook

Dan Atkinson

Salmon House

on the Hill **Cookbook**

Whitecap Books

Vancouver/Toronto/New York

Edited by Elaine Jones
Proofread by Patryce Kidd
Art Direction by Roberta Batchelor
Cover design by Tanya Lloyd/Spotlight Designs
Interior design by Margaret Lee/Bamboo & Silk Design
Front cover photograph by Hot Digital Dog Studios
Interior food photographs by Hot Digital Dog Studios
Other interior photographs by Rob Melnychuk Photography

Printed and bound in Canada

National Library of Canada Cataloguing in Publication Data

Atkinson, Dan.
     Salmon House on the Hill cookbook

     Includes index.
     ISBN 1-55285-004-8

     1. Salmon House on the Hill (Restaurant) 2. Cookery—British
Columbia—West Vancouver. 3. Cookery (Seafood) I. Title.
TX945.5.S24A84 2001   641.5'09711'33   C2001-910483-9

The publisher acknowledges the support of the Canada Council for the Arts and the
Cultural Services Branch of the Government of British Columbia for our publishing
program. We acknowledge the financial support of the Government of Canada through
the Book Publishing Industry Development Program for our publishing activities.

Contents

To my family and everyone else
who helped me with this book.

Introduction

When I was in my early twenties, I stepped into my first restaurant kitchen—not by intent, but driven by circumstance. I headed north and kept going until I ended up in Yellowknife. Famished after weeks of looking for a job, I saw an advertisement in the paper for cooks at the Explorer Hotel. Food sounded pretty good at that point, so I applied for the job.

I fell in love with cooking. The more I learned about ingredients and recipes, the more I wanted to know. After a year in Yellowknife, I moved to Vancouver and attended the Pacific Vocational Institute. Once I had the basics down, I found the world of cooking was mine to explore.

For the past decade I have been keeping the fires warm at the Salmon House on the Hill in West Vancouver, but the restaurant goes back more than a quarter of a century. From the beginning the menu was based on fresh seafood and a traditional style of cooking—grilling over the sweet smoke of alder. This is a technique that brings out the best in many foods. We light the logs each morning and by noon we have the perfect cooking temperature for seafood, about 500°F to 600°F (260°C to 316°C). That allows the salmon, oysters, scallops, halibut, snapper—and whatever else we can lay our hands on—enough time to really soak up that smokiness without getting overdone.

I realize that not everyone has a grill that's 50 cubic feet at home, but as long as you have a barbecue, you can re-create the Salmon House on the Hill experience. Find some alder chips, the greener the better, and soak them in water. Wrap them in tin foil before placing them directly on the coals. Keep the heat low and voilá—you will have the Salmon House in your house.

The original Salmon House on the Hill menu had a few main choices and was based on local foods and traditional dishes such as bannock, chowder and fresh salmon, cheese potatoes and blueberry cobbler. The menu has changed, but certain items are constants. Salmon remains a mainstay of the kitchen. The trademark fiddle-heads and sea asparagus are still served in season as well as the oysters, mussels and clams. But new elements are always being introduced. Star fruit, raspberries, Alaskan black cod, tuna, sea bass—no matter what the ingredients, the end result is a collection of dishes that offer a modernized version of traditional West Coast cuisine. The alder-grilled salmon will never disappear, but I try to toss a little something into the mix to keep things fresh, current and exciting.

When you use this book, bear in mind that no recipe ever tastes the same from one cook to another. The recipe is just a starting point. Everyone brings their own touch, every pair of hands a different interpretation. Then there is the simple issue of availability of particular herbs, produce and meat. We all shop at different markets and this, too, changes the dish.

At home, exercise your freedom to experiment with these recipes. Follow the recipes if you like, but don't be afraid to strike off on a different course and create a culinary hybrid of your own. Add a pinch or a handful whenever the muse moves you. Let your senses and your guests be your guide, and don't forget that cooking is one of the purest forms of expression. Above all else, have fun in the kitchen. I have followed that motto for many years now and it has never done me any harm. Enjoy!

—Dan Atkinson

SALMON HOUSE ON THE HILL RESTAURANT is one of the most enduring culinary landmarks on the West Coast. A sense of history hits you the moment you walk through the door and the smell of the alder-grilled salmon leads you to your table.

With its soaring high-beamed ceilings open to the rafters, the Salmon House bears an architectural resemblance to a traditional long-house design. Over fifty handmade masks gaze down from the walls. The majority of the collection is owned by a North Vancouver resident who started collecting them decades ago and continues to bring new pieces in on a regular basis.

But perhaps the primary reason people are so fascinated by the Salmon House is the salmon. It has always been a staple of the West Coast diet. Just as important, salmon has played a central role in the cultural life of First Nations people on the coast.

The story goes that long ago a race of beings lived in villages beneath the surface of the ocean. They were caretakers who kept the balance between man and nature. Every year they would transform into salmon and swim up the many rivers and streams that pour into the Pacific. Powering themselves over rapids, dodging hungry bears and flying up waterfalls, nothing could deter these magical beings in their quest to maintain balance and feed the people of the coast.

We have done our best to capture the feeling of these traditions in the design of the building and, more importantly, the food itself.

Appetizers

Onion Rings
with Sun-Dried Tomato and Garlic Mayonnaise

Hot sweet onions in a crisp batter are always appealing. You can use this batter with other vegetables, like bell peppers, that can be cut into rings.

16 cups	vegetable oil for frying	4 L
1 cup	flour	240 mL
$1/2$ Tbsp.	baking powder	7.5 mL
$1/2$ Tbsp.	baking soda	7.5 mL
1 cup	cornstarch	240 mL
$1/2$ Tbsp.	salt	7.5 mL
$1/2$ Tbsp.	black pepper	7.5 mL
$1/2$ Tbsp.	lemon pepper	7.5 mL
$1/2$ Tbsp.	garlic powder	7.5 mL
1 Tbsp.	onion flakes	15 mL
	dash cayenne pepper	
1	large egg, slightly beaten	1
2 Tbsp.	vegetable oil	30 mL
1 bottle	12-oz. (341-mL) Tree Amber Ale or other amber ale	1
2	large onions, cut into $1/2$-inch (1.2-cm) slices and separated	2
1 recipe	Sun-Dried Tomato and Garlic Mayonnaise	1 recipe
4 Tbsp.	chopped fresh chives	60 mL

Heat the oil in a deep, heavy, 10-inch (25-cm) frying pan to 350°F (175°C). The depth of oil should be at least 3 inches (7.5 cm), and the pan should be no more than $1/2$ full.

Combine the flour, baking powder, baking soda, cornstarch, salt, black pepper, lemon pepper, garlic powder, onion flakes and cayenne in a bowl. Add the egg, oil and ale and mix together to form a smooth batter.

Dip the onion rings in batter and fry in batches for 5 minutes on each side. Make sure not to crowd too many onion rings in the pan at once. Remove and drain on paper towel. Serve with a dollop of mayonnaise and some chopped chives.

APPETIZERS

Sun-Dried Tomato and Garlic Mayonnaise

MAKES ABOUT 1 $^1/_2$ CUPS (360 ML)		
1 tsp.	rice wine vinegar	5 mL
1	medium egg	1
$^1/_2$ tsp.	salt	2.5 mL
$^1/_2$ tsp.	black pepper	2.5 mL
1 Tbsp.	lemon juice and zest	15 mL
1 Tbsp.	minced garlic	15 mL
$^1/_4$ cup	soft, minced sun-dried tomatoes	60 mL
1 $^1/_3$ cups	vegetable oil	320 mL

Place the vinegar, egg, salt, pepper, lemon juice and zest, garlic and tomatoes in a food processor. With the motor running, slowly add the oil until the mixture is thick. Will keep refrigerated for 3 days.

ROASTING GARLIC

When roasting garlic, slow cooking is the secret. The heads can be sliced in half or left whole. Heat the oven to 375°F (190°C). Without breaking the heads apart, remove as much as you can of the papery coating from 2 heads of garlic. Place the garlic and $^1/_4$ cup (60 mL) water in a small baking dish. Sprinkle with a pinch of salt and 1 Tbsp. (15 mL) olive oil. Cover with aluminum foil and bake, basting with the oil and water mixture after about 30 minutes. Bake until the garlic is soft, about 1 hour. You should be able to pierce it easily with a thin-bladed knife. Roast elephant garlic the same way; it will take a little longer, depending on the size.

Chorizo Quesadilla
with Tomato Salsa and Peppercorn Sour Cream

Quesadillas are great finger foods. Chorizo is a sausage that can be medium or hot; the salsa and sour cream are great garnishes to cool down the spicy chorizos.

2	5-inch (12.5-cm) fresh chorizos	2
$1/4$ cup	minced onion	60 mL
1 tsp.	minced garlic	5 mL
$1/2$ tsp.	sambal oelek	2.5 mL
$1/2$ tsp.	black pepper	2.5 mL
$1/2$ cup	vegetable stock (see page 58)	120 mL
$1/4$ cup	grated Asiago cheese	60 mL
$1/4$ cup	grated Cheddar cheese	60 mL
2	10-inch (25-cm) corn tortillas	2
1 Tbsp.	vegetable oil	15 mL
	salt and black pepper to taste	
$1/4$ cup	sour cream	60 mL
2 Tbsp.	5-peppercorn mix, finely ground	30 mL
1 tsp.	salt	5 mL
1 recipe	Tomato Salsa	1 recipe
2 Tbsp.	chopped fresh chives	30 mL

Split the chorizos in half and remove the sausage meat. Put the meat in a heavy sauté pan and break it up with a fork. Cook over medium heat, rendering out some of the fat, for about 5 minutes. Strain off the fat. Add the onion and garlic and sauté for a couple of minutes. Add the sambal oelek, pepper and stock. Simmer until the stock has been absorbed and the sauce is thick.

Preheat the oven to 400°F (200°C). Sprinkle the Asiago cheese over one of the tortillas. Cover with the sausage mixture and then the Cheddar cheese. Place the other tortilla on top. Carefully brush both sides with oil and dust with salt and pepper. Place on a wire rack on a pizza pan or cookie sheet. Bake in the center of the oven for 5 minutes. Turn it over and bake another 5 minutes. The tortilla should be crisp and the cheese melted.

Remove from the oven and place on a cutting board. Cut into quarters and place on a plate, pulling the quarters apart and leaving an even space between them. Mix the sour cream with the ground pepper mixture and salt in a bowl. Place the sour cream in the middle and top with the salsa. Or you can arrange the quarters on top of each other in a half moon on half the plate, then place the sour cream and salsa side by side on the other half. Either way, sprinkle chopped chives over all.

Tomato Salsa

		MAKES 1 CUP (240 ML)
1	firm tomato	1
1	large tomatillo	1
2 Tbsp.	finely diced red onion	30 mL
3 Tbsp.	chopped green onion	45 mL
1/2 tsp.	diced jalapeño, stem and seeds removed	2.5 mL
1 Tbsp.	chopped cilantro	15 mL
1/4 tsp.	salt	1.2 mL
1/2 tsp.	cracked black pepper	2.5 mL
2 tsp.	lime juice	10 mL
1/2 tsp.	honey	2.5 mL
1/2 Tbsp.	vegetable oil	7.5 mL

Core the tomato and cut it in quarters. Remove the seeds and dice. Husk and coarsely chop the tomatillo. Place the tomatoes, tomatillo, red onion, green onion, jalapeño, cilantro, salt, pepper, lime juice and honey in a bowl. Mix well, add the oil and mix again. Refrigerate until ready to use.

Crab, Potato and Corn Cakes
with Tamarind Sauce and Mango Coulis

For these popular crab cakes, we use local Dungeness crabs—they have the best quality and flavor I have ever tasted. The fresh mango offers a cooling effect on the palate.

1 1/4 lbs.	potatoes, peeled and cut into 2-inch (5-cm) dice	565 g
1/4 cup	butter	60 mL
1/4 cup	minced red onion	60 mL
1 cup	corn niblets	240 mL
1 tsp.	sambal oelek	5 mL
1 Tbsp.	lemon juice	15 mL
1/4 cup	minced green onion	60 mL
2 Tbsp.	minced sweet red pepper	30 mL
4	egg yolks	4
12 oz.	fresh Dungeness crabmeat	340 g
2 Tbsp.	chopped fresh parsley	30 mL
1 tsp.	salt	5 mL
1 1/2 tsp.	black pepper	7.5 mL
1/4 cup	oil	60 mL
3/4 cup	Tamarind Sauce	180 mL
1/2 cup	Mango Coulis	120 mL

Preheat the oven to 350°F (175°C).

Cook the potatoes in salted water, just enough to cover, for about 10 minutes. Drain and spread the potatoes out on a cookie sheet. Dry in the oven for about 5 minutes (you just want to allow the excess water to evaporate). Remove and cool. When they are cool enough to handle, grate them coarsely.

Melt the butter over medium heat. Add the red onion and corn. Sauté for 2 minutes. Add the sambal oelek and lemon juice, and cook for 2 minutes. Add the green onion and red pepper and cook for 2 minutes. Remove from the heat and cool.

Fold the egg yolks into the grated potato. Add the cooled corn mixture and mix in the crabmeat, parsley, salt and pepper. Form into 8 round cakes. Heat the oil in a pan over medium heat and fry the crab cakes until golden brown on both sides, about 5 minutes per side.

Place 3 Tbsp. (45 mL) of the tamarind sauce on each plate. Place 2 crab cakes on top of the sauce and top with 2 Tbsp. (30 mL) of the mango coulis.

Tamarind Sauce

		MAKES 2 CUPS (475 ML)
2 oz.	tamarind paste (see page 85)	57 g
2 Tbsp.	finely minced onion	30 mL
2 tsp.	salt	10 mL
$^1/_2$ tsp.	jalapeño pepper, minced	2.5 mL
$^1/_4$ cup	water	60 mL
$^1/_2$ cup	malt vinegar	120 mL
$^3/_4$ cup	sugar	180 mL
$^1/_4$ cup	mango purée	60 mL
1 tsp.	minced fresh ginger	5 mL
2 Tbsp.	raisins	30 mL

Place all the ingredients in a pot and bring to a boil. Reduce the heat and simmer for 30 minutes, until the texture is like a cream sauce. Break up the tamarind while the mixture is simmering. Keep an eye out for the tamarind seeds and remove them. Leftover sauce will keep for a couple of weeks in the refrigerator. You can add this sauce to curries and soups or use it to top meat, fish or chicken.

Mango Coulis

		MAKES 1 $^1/_2$ CUPS (360 ML)
1 cup	diced fresh mango, skin and seed removed	240 mL
$^1/_2$ cup	water	120 mL

Place the water in a blender and add half of the mango. Purée the mixture, slowly adding the rest of the mango until the mixture is thick and smooth.

It can be kept in the fridge for up to a week. Leftover coulis can be mixed with salad dressing or ketchup. It can also be frozen in ice cube trays and served as sorbet, especially nice with Champagne.

Pork Spring Rolls
with Warm Swiss Chard and Sesame Seed Dressing

Crispy wrappers filled with tasty filling are a real favorite with everyone. These can be prepared a day ahead and then cooked as you need them.

FOR THE MARINATED PORK:

1/3 cup	ketchup	80 mL
1/3 cup	soy sauce	80 mL
1 tsp.	Dijon mustard	5 mL
1 Tbsp.	Worcestershire sauce	15 mL
1/2 tsp.	sambal oelek	2.5 mL
6 oz.	pork tenderloin	170 g

Mix the ketchup, soy sauce, mustard, Worcestershire sauce and sambal oelek together. Cut the pork into 1/4-inch (.6-cm) slices and marinate overnight in the mixture. Pan-fry or grill the pork for 2 minutes per side. Allow to cool before slicing into thin, match-like strips.

TO ASSEMBLE THE SPRING ROLLS:

1/4 cup	minced sweet red pepper	60 mL
1/4 cup	minced onion	60 mL
1/4 cup	scallions, sliced thin	60 mL
1/4 cup	grated carrot	60 mL
2 Tbsp.	lemon pepper	30 mL
2 Tbsp.	soy sauce	30 mL
8	8-inch (20-cm) spring roll wrappers	8
1	egg, slightly beaten	1

Mix the cooked pork with the sweet red pepper, onion, scallion, carrot, lemon pepper and soy sauce. Divide the mixture into 8 and put a portion in the center of each wrapper. Spread the mix into a diagonal line about 5 inches (12.5 cm) long. Brush the edges of the wrapper with the egg wash and fold the 2 points in towards the mix. Brush with egg wash again and roll it up tight.

To fry the spring rolls, pour oil into a 10-inch (25-cm) heavy pot to a depth of 4 inches (10 cm). Heat oil to 350°F (175°C). Fry 2 at a time for about 5 minutes each. They should be crisp and golden brown. Drain on paper towel and keep warm.

TO SERVE:

8	leaves red Swiss chard, stem removed	8
1 Tbsp.	sesame oil	15 mL
3 Tbsp.	olive oil	45 mL
1 Tbsp.	cracked black pepper	15 mL
1 recipe	Sesame Seed Dressing	1 recipe

Slice the chard into 1-inch (2.5-cm) strips and toss with the oils and cracked black pepper. Sauté over medium heat for 1 minute, just to wilt. Divide evenly among 4 plates. Place 2 spring rolls over the chard and top each with 4 Tbsp. (60 mL) of the dressing.

Sesame Seed Dressing

		MAKES 1 CUP (240 ML)
4	large egg yolks	4
1 Tbsp.	lemon juice	15 mL
1 Tbsp.	soy sauce	15 mL
$^1/_2$ tsp.	salt	2.5 mL
2 Tbsp.	white wine	30 mL
4 tsp.	Dijon mustard	20 mL
1 tsp.	minced garlic	5 mL
1 tsp.	white pepper	5 mL
$^1/_2$ cup	vegetable oil	120 mL
2 Tbsp.	sesame oil	30 mL
2 Tbsp.	chopped scallions	30 mL

Mix together the egg yolks, lemon juice, soy sauce, salt, white wine, mustard, garlic and pepper. Combine the oils and slowly whisk into the egg yolk mixture. Mix in the scallions. Refrigerate for up to 3 days.

Piri-Piri Grilled Pork
with Tamarind Chipotle Sauce

Piri-piri means hot-hot. The chile pepper in question here is one of the smallest members of the capsicum family—and it has a ferocious bite. You can substitute cayenne pepper.

1/4 cup	oil	60 mL
2 Tbsp.	minced garlic	30 mL
2 Tbsp.	minced fresh ginger	30 mL
1 Tbsp.	cayenne pepper	15 mL
1 tsp.	sambal oelek	5 mL
1/3 cup	lime juice	80 mL
1 tsp.	salt	5 mL
1 tsp.	black pepper	5 mL
8	4-oz. (113-g) pork chops	8
1 recipe	Tamarind Chipotle Sauce	1 recipe

Heat the oil in a small pan over low heat, add the garlic and sauté until it is soft. Do not allow it to brown. Set aside to cool. Mix the ginger, cayenne, sambal oelek, lime juice, salt and pepper in a small bowl. Whisk in the garlic oil. Pour the mixture over the pork chops. Cover and refrigerate for 4 hours.

Heat a grill to medium-high and cook the chops for 20 minutes, turning frequently and basting with the marinade. Serve immediately with the sauce.

Tamarind Chipotle Sauce

	MAKES 2 CUPS (475 ML)	
7 oz.	tamarind paste (see page 85)	200 g
1 1/2 cups	water	360 mL
1/4 cup	Demerara sugar	60 mL
1 Tbsp.	roasted garlic (see page 13)	15 mL
1	chipotle pepper in adobo sauce	1
1/2	lime, juice only	1/2

Cut the tamarind paste into small pieces and add it to the water. Bring to a simmer. Add the sugar, garlic, chili and lime juice. Stir until smooth. Remove any seeds and transfer to a blender. Process until the mixture is smooth. Serve at room temperature.

Beef Tenderloin Slices
with Wild West Barbecue Sauce

This barbecue sauce originated in Windsor, Ontario, where it was called tunnel barbecue sauce. It has been adapted for West Coast tastes.

1/2 cup	ketchup	120 mL
1/3 cup	prepared mustard	80 mL
2 1/2 Tbsp.	red wine vinegar	37.5 mL
3 Tbsp.	sugar	45 mL
1 tsp.	garlic powder	5 mL
	pinch cayenne pepper	
1 tsp.	salt	5 mL
1 tsp.	lemon pepper	5 mL
2 tsp.	Mexican chili powder	10 mL
4 tsp.	minced onion	20 mL
8	2-oz. (57-g) slices beef tenderloin	8
4	leaves butter lettuce	4
1/4 cup	diced, seeded tomatoes	60 mL

Mix the ketchup, mustard, vinegar, sugar, garlic powder, cayenne, salt, lemon pepper, chili powder and onion together. Let sit for 30 minutes. Add the beef and marinate overnight in the refrigerator.

Heat the grill to medium-high. Cook the beef for about 2 minutes on each side for rare, longer if you like it medium or well done. Brush the beef with the marinade two or three times during cooking. Place a lettuce leaf on each plate and top with 2 slices of beef. Place a spoonful of diced tomato on the beef and serve.

APPETIZERS

Chicken and Leek Risotto
with Tomato Chipotle Pepper Jus

In the restaurant, we cook the risotto halfway and quickly chill it, which speeds up the cooking time, but this is certainly not necessary. The spicy chipotle pepper complements the richness of the dish.

2 Tbsp.	olive oil	30 mL
1 cup	minced onion	240 mL
1 1/3 cups	Arborio rice	320 mL
2 tsp.	minced garlic	10 mL
3 Tbsp.	dry sherry	45 mL
4 cups	hot chicken or vegetable stock (see page 57 or 58)	1 L
8 oz.	boneless skinless chicken, cut into 1/2-inch (1.2-cm) dice	225 g
1/2 cup	chopped leeks, white part only	120 mL
1/2 tsp.	salt	2.5 mL
1/2 tsp.	black pepper	2.5 mL
1/2 cup	grated Cheddar cheese	120 mL
1/2 cup	Tomato Chipotle Pepper Jus, warmed	120 mL

Heat the oil in a large, heavy pan over medium-high heat. Add the onion and cook for 1 minute. Do not allow the onion to color. Stir in the rice and cook for 1 minute.

Add the garlic and sherry. Stir in about 1/3 of the stock and bring to a simmer. Stir the rice constantly for even cooking and to make sure it doesn't burn on the bottom. Add the chicken, leeks, salt and pepper.

When the stock has been almost completely absorbed, about 5 minutes, add another 1/3 of the stock. Return to a simmer and cook another 5 to 10 minutes, until the stock is absorbed. Add the last of the stock and half the cheese. Bring to a simmer and cook for 5 to 10 more minutes. When the stock is completely absorbed the risotto is done.

Remove from the heat and divide between two bowls. Top with the rest of the cheese and spoon 1/4 cup (60 mL) of the jus around the rice in each bowl.

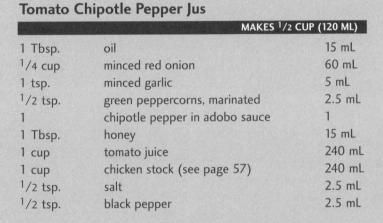

Tomato Chipotle Pepper Jus

		MAKES $^1/_2$ CUP (120 ML)
1 Tbsp.	oil	15 mL
$^1/_4$ cup	minced red onion	60 mL
1 tsp.	minced garlic	5 mL
$^1/_2$ tsp.	green peppercorns, marinated	2.5 mL
1	chipotle pepper in adobo sauce	1
1 Tbsp.	honey	15 mL
1 cup	tomato juice	240 mL
1 cup	chicken stock (see page 57)	240 mL
$^1/_2$ tsp.	salt	2.5 mL
$^1/_2$ tsp.	black pepper	2.5 mL

Heat the oil in a pot over medium heat. Add the onion and cook until golden, about 2 minutes. Add the garlic, peppercorns, chipotle pepper, honey, tomato juice, stock, salt and pepper. Bring to a simmer and cook until reduced to $^1/_2$ cup (120 mL). This should take about 10 minutes. Cool down and liquefy in a blender.

Potato Baguette
with Green Olive Tapenade

Served with a tomato juice, a Caesar cocktail or a glass of red wine, these morsels get any event off to a great start. There is more tapenade than you need. It will last up to 2 weeks in the fridge and can be used not only as a spread, but as a dip for raw vegetables, sandwich spread or an ingredient in a salad dressing.

1 cup	pimento-stuffed green olives	240 mL
3	oil-packed anchovy fillets	3
1 Tbsp.	lemon juice	15 mL
1 tsp.	minced garlic	5 mL
	pinch red chili flakes	
1/4 cup	fresh basil, packed	60 mL
2 Tbsp.	olive oil	30 mL
1	potato baguette, about 12 inches (30 cm) long, cut into 1-inch (2.5-cm) slices	1
1/4 cup	butter at room temperature (optional)	60 mL
4	sprigs fresh parsley	4

Place the olives, anchovies, lemon juice, garlic and chili flakes in a food processor and process until coarsely chopped. Transfer to a mixing bowl. Finely chop the basil and add to the mix. Add the olive oil a little at a time until it is mixed in. Cover and refrigerate.

Butter the bread, if desired, and spread 1 Tbsp. (15 mL) tapenade on each slice. Top with a parsley sprig.

Crab, Potato and Corn Cakes with
Tamarind Sauce and Mango Coulis
(page 16)

Moon with Four Seasons Crest
by George Pennier

View from the Salmon House on the Hill
overlooking Lions Gate Bridge and Vancouver

Mesclun Greens and Beet Chips
(page 62)

Smoked Salmon Roulade

This is a light and colorful way of serving salmon. We serve it cold but it can also be served hot. We call it roulade because of the way it is rolled up, somewhat in the style of beef roulade.

1 lb.	spinach, washed and trimmed	455 g
1 cup	Parmesan cheese	240 mL
6	eggs, separated	6
$^1/_2$ tsp.	salt	2.5 mL
$^1/_2$ tsp.	black pepper	2.5 mL
$^3/_4$ cup	cream cheese	180 mL
1 tsp.	chopped fresh dill	5 mL
1 tsp.	chopped fresh basil	5 mL
1 Tbsp.	lemon juice	15 mL
10 oz.	sliced smoked salmon	285 g

Preheat the oven to 350°F (175°C). Line a 12 x 15-inch (30 x 38-cm) cookie sheet with parchment paper.

Blanch the spinach in salted boiling water for 1 minute. Place under cold water to chill, then squeeze out as much water as possible. Chop the spinach and put it in a food processor. Add the cheese, egg yolks, salt and pepper. Pulse until well mixed and remove to a bowl.

Beat the egg whites to the stiff peak stage. Fold the spinach mixture into the egg whites. Spread the mixture evenly onto the prepared pan. Bake for 10 minutes. Remove from the oven and cool.

Place the cream cheese, dill, basil and lemon juice in the food processor. Pulse until smooth and spreadable. Spread the herbed cream cheese over the spinach soufflé. Place the smoked salmon on the cream cheese. Roll it up like a jelly roll and cut it into slices. You can serve it right away or refrigerate it for up to 3 or 4 days.

APPETIZERS

Candied Salmon

How can you make something better? Candy it! You can use the whole salmon fillet, but the salmon bellies contain the most oil and will give a richer dish.

1 lb.	trimmed salmon bellies	455 g
1 cup	soy sauce	240 mL
1 cup	brown sugar	240 mL
1/2 cup	white sugar	120 mL
1 Tbsp.	sesame oil	15 mL
1/4 cup	plum wine	60 mL
2 tsp.	minced garlic	10 mL
2 tsp.	minced fresh ginger	10 mL
1/2 tsp.	salt	2.5 mL
2 tsp.	lemon pepper	10 mL
1/4 cup	maple syrup	60 mL

Wash the salmon and pat it dry. Combine all the other ingredients and pour over the salmon. Stir to make sure it is well coated with the marinade. Refrigerate and marinate for 2 days, stirring every 12 hours.

Remove the salmon from the marinade. If you have a smoker, smoke it for 2 hours at 80°F to 100°F (27°C to 38°C). Slow cooking on your barbecue works just as well. Heat it to low and cook the salmon for 2 hours. Add a few wood chips for extra flavor. I find that greener wood creates more smoke and that is good. If the wood chips are dry, soak them in water for 10 minutes before putting them on. Remember that they burn up fast, so put a little on at a time to make the smoke last the whole cooking time. A third method is to bake the salmon in the oven at 275°F (135°C) for about 1 hour.

Smoked Sockeye Salmon Cheesecake

This is a good recipe for a cheese appetizer. It can be served warm right from the oven or chilled from the refrigerator. The smoked sockeye salmon adds a rich, smooth, smoky flavor.

$1/2$ cup	grated Parmesan cheese	120 mL
2 Tbsp.	butter	30 mL
$1/2$ cup	minced onion	120 mL
$1/2$ tsp.	minced garlic	2.5 mL
1 $1/2$ lbs.	cream cheese	680 g
4	eggs	4
$1/2$ cup	whipping cream	120 mL
$1/2$ lb.	smoked salmon, puréed	225 g

Preheat the oven to 300°F (150°C). Line a 4 x 12-inch (10 x 30-cm) pan with parchment paper. Brush with butter and sprinkle with a little of the Parmesan cheese.

Melt the butter in a sauté pan over medium heat. Add the onion and garlic and sauté for about 2 minutes. Do not allow them to color. Remove from the heat and set aside to cool.

Place the cream cheese in a food processor and pulse until smooth. Add the eggs, cream and salmon and process slowly on low speed until it is well mixed. Pour into the pan and sprinkle with the remaining Parmesan cheese.

Place the pan in a larger pan and add enough water to come halfway up the side of the pan with the cheesecake. Bake for 1 $1/2$ hours. Cool, then chill in the refrigerator for at least 2 hours or overnight. It slices well when chilled, but it does get firmer the longer it chills.

APPETIZERS

Salmon in Buttermilk Ale Batter
with Pacific Wave Tartar Sauce

Dipping the salmon in the batter first and then in the flour gives a slightly different texture to the finished batter.

1 cup	flour	240 mL
2 cups	buttermilk	475 mL
1 cup	Okanagan Spring Pale Ale or other pale ale	240 mL
	pinch cayenne pepper	
1 tsp.	salt	5 mL
1/4 cup	minced onion	60 mL
12	2-oz. (57-g) boneless skinless salmon fillets	12
4 cups	oil	1 L
2 cups	flour	475 mL
8	lemon wedges	8
1 recipe	Pacific Wave Tartar Sauce	1 recipe

Combine the flour, buttermilk, ale, cayenne, salt and onion. Don't overmix. Soak the salmon in the batter for 2 hours.

Heat the oil to 350°F (175°C) in a deep, heavy pot. Dredge the salmon in the flour. Fry the salmon in batches so they are not overcrowded. Fry each batch for about 5 minutes. Drain on paper towels. Serve with lemon wedges and tartar sauce.

Pacific Wave Tartar Sauce

		MAKES 1 CUP (240 ML)
2 Tbsp.	mayonnaise (see page 178)	30 mL
2 Tbsp.	sour cream	30 mL
2 Tbsp.	plain yogurt	30 mL
1 Tbsp.	capers, drained	15 mL
1 Tbsp.	minced onion	15 mL
1 tsp.	chopped fresh parsley	5 mL
1 tsp.	grated horseradish	5 mL
1 tsp.	Greek olives, pits removed, washed, chopped	5 mL
1 tsp.	stuffed green olives	5 mL
2 Tbsp.	hamburger or hot dog relish	30 mL
	dash Worcestershire sauce	
	dash hot pepper sauce	
$1/2$ cup	ketchup	120 mL
1 tsp.	lemon juice	5 mL
	pinch salt and black pepper	

Place everything in a bowl and mix well. Keep refrigerated. If the mayonnaise is fresh, the tartar sauce will keep in the fridge for 3 days.

Sockeye Salmon Corn Dog
with Mustard Dill Aïoli

This dish is always a hit because it is so much fun to make and eat. You will need 10 bamboo skewers, 6 inches (15 cm) long, soaked in water. Soaking the skewers stops them from splintering when skewering the salmon.

1 cup	cornmeal	240 mL
1/3 cup	cornstarch	80 mL
3/4 cup	flour	180 mL
1/2 tsp.	baking powder	2.5 mL
1 tsp.	salt	5 mL
1 tsp.	black pepper	5 mL
1 1/4 cups	buttermilk	300 mL
10	2-oz. (57-g) strips of boneless skinless sockeye salmon, about 5 inches (12.5 cm) long and 1/2 inch (1.2 cm) wide	10
1 recipe	Mustard Dill Aïoli	1 recipe
1/4 cup	chopped fresh chives	60 mL

Mix together the cornmeal, cornstarch, flour, baking powder, salt and pepper in a bowl. Make a well and stir in the buttermilk with a wooden spoon. Do not overmix. Let the batter sit for half an hour.

While the batter is resting, thread the salmon on the skewers. Dip the salmon into the batter, making sure the salmon is completely covered. Heat 4 cups (1 L) oil in a heavy 8-inch (20-cm) pot until it reaches 350°F (175°C). Deep-fry the battered salmon for 5 to 8 minutes. Drain on a paper towel.

Dip the salmon skewers into the aïoli, making sure one side is coated. Sprinkle with a few chives.

Mustard Dill Aïoli

		MAKES 1 1/2 CUPS (360 ML)
3	egg yolks	3
2 Tbsp.	Dijon mustard	30 mL
1/2 tsp.	minced garlic	2.5 mL
1/2 tsp.	salt	2.5 mL
1/2 tsp.	black pepper	2.5 mL
1 Tbsp.	lemon juice	15 mL
3 Tbsp.	chopped fresh dill	45 mL
3/4 cup	olive oil	180 mL

In a small bowl mix together the egg yolks, mustard, garlic, salt, pepper, lemon juice and dill. Slowly whisk in the olive oil. Refrigerate until you need it; it will keep for up to 3 days.

Hot Smoked Salmon
with Warm Horseradish Cream and Spicy Cornbread

Hot smoking gives a dryer effect and a smokier taste for the salmon. It's not quite as dry as a jerk but it has a similar flavor.

4 Tbsp.	butter	60 mL
1/2 cup	minced onion	120 mL
1/2 cup	fresh horseradish, peeled and grated	120 mL
2 cups	whipping cream	475 mL
1/2 tsp.	salt	2.5 mL
1/2 tsp.	black pepper	2.5 mL
1 tsp.	sugar	5 mL
1/2 tsp.	lemon juice	2.5 mL
1 lb.	hot smoked salmon, unsliced	455 g

Heat the butter in a medium saucepan until it bubbles. Add the onion and horseradish and sauté for 1 minute. Add the cream. Bring to a simmer and cook until reduced by half. Add the salt, pepper, sugar and lemon juice.

Barbecue the smoked salmon for 10 minutes over medium heat. Cut into 4 pieces, top with a little sauce and serve with the warm cornbread.

Spicy Cornbread

		MAKES 1 LOAF
1 cup	flour	240 mL
2 Tbsp.	sugar	30 mL
1 Tbsp.	baking powder	15 mL
1 tsp.	salt	5 mL
1/2 tsp.	chili powder	2.5 mL
	pinch black pepper	
1 cup	cornmeal	240 mL
1 tsp.	crushed chillies	5 mL
2 Tbsp.	chilled butter	30 mL
1/4 cup	grated Parmesan cheese	60 mL
1/4 cup	grated Cheddar cheese	60 mL
1/4 cup	grated Swiss cheese	60 mL
1/4 cup	sweet red bell pepper, stem and seeds removed	60 mL
1	jalapeño pepper, stem and seeds removed	1
1 cup	buttermilk	240 mL
2	eggs, lightly beaten	2

Preheat the oven to 350°F (175°C). Line a 5 x 9-inch (12.5 x 23-cm) loaf pan with silicon or parchment paper.

Sift the flour, sugar, baking powder, salt, chili powder and black pepper into a bowl. Stir in the cornmeal and crushed chilies. Grate in the butter and mix well. Add the grated cheeses and mix well.

Purée the peppers and combine with the buttermilk and eggs. Fold the mixture into the dry ingredients. Do not overmix. Pour the batter into the pan and smooth the top. The pan should be almost full. Bake in the center of the oven for 1 hour, rotating the pan halfway through the baking time so it will cook evenly. Cool slightly in the pan, then remove the loaf and cool on a rack.

Barbecued Oysters
with Jalapeño, Mushroom and Bacon Vinaigrette

The oysters are served hot in this dish and the vinaigrette cool, although it has its own heat. We use local Fanny Bay oysters that are about 2 years old, but any oysters can be used. You will have about 3 cups (720 mL) of vinaigrette. It will keep in the fridge for a week and is delicious with salads or fish. It will thicken in the fridge because of the oil so let it sit at room temperature before using.

6 Tbsp.	olive oil	90 mL
16	fresh oysters, shucked	16
8	slices barbecued double-smoked bacon, cut into 1/2-inch (1.2-cm) dice	8
1 1/2 cups	diced mushrooms	360 mL
1 cup	diced red onion	240 mL
1 Tbsp.	minced garlic	15 mL
2	jalapeño peppers, stem and seeds removed, minced	2
1 Tbsp.	chopped fresh thyme	15 mL
1/2 Tbsp.	salt	7.5 mL
1/2 Tbsp.	black pepper	7.5 mL
1 Tbsp.	sambal oelek	15 mL
1 1/2 cups	malt vinegar	360 mL
1/4 cup	olive oil	60 mL
1	lemon, juiced	1
	dash hot pepper sauce	
	salt and black pepper to taste	
1/2	lemon, cut in wedges	1/2

Heat the 6 Tbsp. (90 mL) oil in a pan over medium heat. Add the bacon, mushrooms and onion and sauté until brown. Add the jalapeño pepper, thyme, salt, pepper and sambal oelek. Remove from the heat and add the malt vinegar. Cool to room temperature.

Toss the oysters with the 1/4 cup (60 mL) olive oil, lemon juice, hot pepper sauce, salt and pepper. Place in a pan over medium-high heat and cook for 5 minutes per side, or less if you prefer them a little underdone. Divide the oysters among 4 plates. Spoon 2 Tbsp. (30 mL) of vinaigrette over each serving and serve with a wedge of lemon.

Oysters on the Half Shell
with Artichoke, Shallot and Apple Cider Mignonette

Our West Coast oysters are known for their deep, cup-shaped shells—used to good advantage in this presentation.

12	fresh oysters	12
2 Tbsp.	minced onion	30 mL
4 Tbsp.	minced canned artichokes	60 mL
1 tsp.	lemon juice	5 mL
6 Tbsp.	apple cider vinegar	90 mL
6 Tbsp.	dry white wine	90 mL
1/2 tsp.	black pepper	2.5 mL
	pinch cayenne pepper	
2	lemon wedges	2

Scrub the oysters in the shell. Shuck the oysters and arrange them in the deep half of the shells on a bed of ice. Mix the onion, artichoke, lemon juice, vinegar, wine, pepper and cayenne together in a bowl. Set aside for at least 5 minutes.

Either serve the mignonette on the side or place 1/2 tsp. (2.5 mL) on each oyster. Serve with the lemon wedges.

Oysters on the Half Shell
with Wasabi Tobiko and Champagne

Flying fish roe are the eggs that you usually see on California rolls. When they are infused with wasabi, they are bright green and are called wasabi tobiko. You can purchase wasabi tobiko already made. Ask for it at your specialty fish store. This is a great blend of flavors.

24	fresh oysters	24
1/2 cup	wasabi tobiko	120 mL
1 cup	Champagne	240 mL

Scrub the oysters in the shell under running water. Shuck the oysters just before serving and save the liquor that spills from the shell. Strain the liquor through a fine sieve.

Arrange the oysters in their deep shells on a bed of ice, and pour the liquor over them. Place 1 tsp. (5 mL) of the wasabi tobiko over each of the oysters and top with about 2 tsp. (10 mL) of Champagne. Serve immediately.

Oyster and Potato Jacks
with Pancetta Remoulade

16	raw oysters, shucked	16
1/2 cup	butter	120 mL
4 cups	mashed potatoes	1 L
4	green onions, chopped	4
2 Tbsp.	chopped fresh dill	30 mL
2 tsp.	salt	10 mL
1 Tbsp.	lemon pepper	15 mL
2 Tbsp.	flour	30 mL
1 recipe	Pancetta Remoulade	1 recipe

Pat the oysters dry. Heat 1/4 cup (60 mL) of the butter in a frying pan over medium heat and add the oysters. Cook the oysters, turning them to brown on all sides.

Let the oysters cool and cut them in half. Mix the mashed potatoes, green onions, dill, salt, lemon pepper and flour. Carefully fold in the oysters. Form the mixture into 3-inch (7.5-cm) patties and fry until golden brown in the remaining 1/4 cup (60 mL) butter. Top each patty with a dollop of the remoulade.

Pancetta Remoulade

	MAKES 1 CUP (240 ML)	
3/4 cup	mayonnaise	180 mL
1 Tbsp.	capers	15 mL
2 Tbsp.	diced cooked pancetta	30 mL
1 Tbsp.	minced onion	15 mL
1/2 tsp.	minced garlic	2.5 mL
1 Tbsp.	chopped fresh dill	15 mL
1 Tbsp.	chopped fresh basil	15 mL
1 Tbsp.	chopped fresh parsley	15 mL
	pinch salt	
1/2 tsp.	black pepper	2.5 mL
1 Tbsp.	lemon, juice and zest	15 mL
1 Tbsp.	minced jalapeño pepper	15 mL
3	anchovy fillets, chopped	3

Mix everything together and refrigerate until needed.

APPETIZERS

Sautéed Oysters
with Peppered Spinach and Nutmeg Cream

This is a comforting dish on a rainy winter day. It goes well with a loaf of crusty bread.

12	medium-sized oysters, shucked	12
3 Tbsp.	flour	45 mL
1 tsp.	salt	5 mL
1 tsp.	black pepper	5 mL
1/2 cup	butter	120 mL
1/4 cup	minced onion	60 mL
2 Tbsp.	minced celery	30 mL
1 tsp.	grated nutmeg	5 mL
1/4 cup	white wine	60 mL
1 1/2 cups	heavy cream	360 mL
1/4 cup	chopped fresh chives	60 mL
1/4 cup	olive oil	60 mL
1 lb.	spinach, washed and trimmed	455 g
1/2 tsp.	salt	2.5 mL
1 Tbsp.	cracked black pepper	15 mL

Lightly dust the oysters with flour and half the salt and black pepper. Heat the butter over medium heat in a heavy pan until it starts to bubble. Add the oysters and cook for 2 minutes. Turn the oysters over, add the onion, celery and nutmeg, and cook for another 2 minutes.

Add the white wine. When the mixture comes to a simmer, remove the oysters and add the cream. Simmer and stir until it is reduced by half. Return the oysters to the pan and add the remaining 1/2 tsp. (2.5 mL) salt and black pepper and the chives. Simmer until the sauce is thick and the oysters are firm to the touch, about 5 minutes. Remove from the heat.

In a large flat pan, heat the oil just until it starts to smoke. Add the spinach. Toss once and add the 1/2 tsp. (2.5 mL) salt and cracked pepper. Divide among 4 plates. Top with the oysters and sauce.

Clams

with Gin, Ginger and Scallions

I was talking with some regulars in our dining room at lunch one day, and they told me that I wouldn't have lived until I'd had clams with gin and ginger. Well, I tried it, and here it is to share with you.

3 lbs.	clams, scrubbed and purged	1.35 kg
1 Tbsp.	vegetable oil	15 mL
1/4 cup	minced ginger	60 mL
1/2 cup	minced onion	120 mL
1 cup	ginger wine	240 mL
3/4 cup	gin	180 mL
1 tsp.	salt	5 mL
1 1/2 tsp.	black pepper	7.5 mL
1 cup	green onions, chopped	240 mL
4 Tbsp.	butter	60 mL

Dry the clams. Place a heavy 16-cup (4-L) pot with a lid over medium-high heat and add the oil. Heat until the oil smokes. Add the clams, cover and cook for 2 minutes. Add the ginger, onion, ginger wine, gin, salt, pepper and onions. Cover again and cook for 5 minutes. Check to see if all the clams are open and discard any that haven't opened. Add the butter, stir gently and serve with fresh bread.

PURGING CLAMS

Clams burrow in sand, and sometimes get a few grains of sand inside the shell. To purge clams of sand, cover them with water in a large pot and add 1 Tbsp. (15 mL) salt and 1 Tbsp. (15 mL) cornmeal. Let them sit for 2 hours, stirring gently every half hour so the cornmeal doesn't stay on the bottom. Adding the salt makes the clams feel like at home—like being in the salty ocean. The theory is that the clams will take in the cornmeal and then spit it out with the sand. It seems to work for us.

APPETIZERS

Spicy Clams
with Coconut, Lime Broth and Carrot Spaghettini

This is a classic combination of flavors. The long strands of carrot add color and give the dish a pasta-like texture.

2–3	jumbo carrots	2–3
4 Tbsp.	vegetable oil	60 mL
4	large shallots, chopped	4
4 tsp.	minced fresh ginger	20 mL
1 tsp.	ground turmeric	5 mL
1 tsp.	cumin seed	5 mL
3 lbs.	clams, scrubbed and purged (see page 39)	1.35 kg
2 cups	clam nectar	475 mL
1 cup	coconut milk	240 mL
1 cup	tomato concasse (see page 99)	240 mL
4 tsp.	minced jalapeño peppers	20 mL
1 tsp.	grated lime zest	5 mL
4 Tbsp.	lime juice	60 mL
1 tsp.	salt	5 mL
1 tsp.	black pepper	5 mL
4	chopped green onions	4

Peel the carrots and slice them lengthwise as thin as you can. (A mandoline works well for this). Cut each slice into long, thin strips like spaghettini. Cook the strips in rapidly boiling salted water for 1 minute. Strain and chill under cool running water. Drain well. You should have about 2 cups (475 mL).

Place the oil in a heavy 16-cup (4-L) pot over medium heat. When the oil is hot, sauté the shallots for 2 minutes. Add the ginger, turmeric, cumin, clams, clam nectar, coconut milk, tomatoes, jalapeño and lime zest. Bring to a boil, cover and cook for 5 minutes. Check the clams and remove any that haven't opened. Add the lime juice, salt and pepper. Divide the clams among 4 bowls and top each with the carrot spaghettini and green onions.

Blue Mussels

with Baby Shrimp, Tomatoes, Basil and Cream

We love mussels here in Vancouver, but I understand that in Brussels they are the national food and are served with French fries on the side. Mussels and shrimp go very well together and lean towards being on the aphrodisiac side of cooking.

1/2 cup	vegetable oil	120 mL
3 lbs.	mussels, washed and bearded	1.35 kg
1/2 cup	minced onion	120 mL
2 tsp.	minced garlic	10 mL
1/4 cup	lemon juice	60 mL
1 cup	white wine	240 mL
1/2 cup	chopped fresh basil	120 mL
4	tomatoes, seeds and stem removed, chopped	4
1/2 tsp.	salt	2.5 mL
2 tsp.	black pepper	10 mL
1/2 lb.	baby shrimp	225 g
2 cups	whipping cream	475 mL

Heat the oil in a heavy 16-cup (4-L) pot over medium heat. Add the mussels, onion, garlic, lemon juice, wine, basil, tomato, salt and pepper. Increase the heat to high and add the shrimp and cream. Cook until the mussels are open, about 5 minutes.

PREPARING MUSSELS

Discard any mussels with shells that do not close when the inside is prodded. Scrape or rub off any encrusting growth. Remove the beard (the attached fibers) with a quick pull. Wash under cold running water. If the mussels are from a sandy area, soak them in salted water—1 1/2 Tbsp. (22.5 mL) salt to 4 cups (1 L) water—for 30 to 60 minutes, changing the water every 15 minutes. The characteristic color of mussel meat is bright orange when cooked. The entire inside is edible.

APPETIZERS

41

Salt Roasted Mussels
with Malt Vinegar Aïoli

Only here can you buy mussels that are more expensive than the ones flown in from 4,000 miles (6,500 km) away. We sometimes use Saltspring Island mussels because they are smaller than East Coast mussels, and they are local.

3 lbs.	mussels, washed and bearded (see page 41)	1.35 kg
1/2 cup	rock salt	120 mL
1/4 cup	malt vinegar	60 mL
1 tsp.	lemon juice	5 mL
3	egg yolks	3
1/2 tsp.	minced garlic	2.5 mL
1/2 tsp.	salt	2.5 mL
1/2 tsp.	black pepper	2.5 mL
1 cup	olive oil	240 mL

Preheat the oven to 500°F (260°C).

Drain any excess water from the mussels. Place them close together in a single layer in an ovenproof dish. Sprinkle the salt over the mussels. Bake for 5 minutes, until the mussels are open. In a mixing bowl, combine the vinegar, lemon juice, egg yolks, garlic, salt and pepper. Slowly add the olive oil, whisking until it has become a thick, mayonnaise-like sauce.

Divide the mussels among 4 bowls. Serve the aïoli over the mussels or serve it separately as a dipping sauce.

Yam Fries
with Curried Shrimp

Starches go very well with curry. This is like having fries with gravy—and since you are at a seafood restaurant, we add some shrimp.

2 Tbsp.	oil or butter	30 mL
1 Tbsp.	minced onion	15 mL
1/2 tsp.	minced garlic	2.5 mL
1/2 tsp.	minced fresh ginger	2.5 mL
1/2 tsp.	salt	2.5 mL
1/2 tsp.	curry powder	2.5 mL
	pinch ground cumin, coriander, garam marsala, cinnamon, pepper and turmeric	
6 oz.	baby shrimp	170 g
1 Tbsp.	chopped seeded tomato	15 mL
1 Tbsp.	chopped green onion	15 mL
1 tsp.	chopped cilantro	5 mL
1/2 cup	vegetable stock (see page 58)	120 mL
2 lbs.	yams	900 g
4 cups	vegetable oil	1 L
	pinch salt and black pepper	

Heat the 2 Tbsp. (30 mL) oil or butter in a sauté pan over medium heat. Add the onion, garlic, ginger, salt, curry and ground spices and cook for 1 minute. Add the shrimp and toss. Add the tomato, green onion, cilantro and stock. Cook for 3 to 5 minutes, until the sauce is thick. Keep warm.

Cut the yams into 1/4 x 4-inch (.6 x 10-cm) batons. Heat the oil in a deep, heavy pot to 350°F (175°C). Add the yams and cook for 3 to 5 minutes. I like the yams a little underdone and golden brown. Remove and place on a paper towel to drain. Dust with salt and pepper. Place the fries in a bowl and top with the curried shrimp.

Sautéed Tiger Prawns
with Peanuts, Grapes and Lime Juice

There are so many textures and flavors in this recipe that it appeals to almost all tastes!

4 Tbsp.	clarified butter	60 mL
20	tiger prawns, peeled and deveined (see page 121)	20
4 Tbsp.	minced onion	60 mL
1 tsp.	minced garlic	5 mL
$^1/_2$ cup	roasted peanuts	120 mL
1 Tbsp.	sambal oelek	15 mL
1	lime, juice only	1
1 cup	red seedless grapes, cut in half	240 mL
4 Tbsp.	chopped scallions	60 mL
$^1/_2$ tsp.	salt	2.5 mL
$^1/_2$ tsp.	black pepper	2.5 mL
4 Tbsp.	chilled butter, diced	60 mL

Heat the clarified butter in a 10-inch (25-cm) frying pan over high heat. Add the prawns, then the onion and garlic. As soon as the onion starts to brown, toss the mixture and add the peanuts and sambal oelek. Add the lime juice, toss, and add the grapes, scallions, salt and pepper. Add the diced butter, swirling the pan until it is just melted. Divide evenly into 4 portions and serve with a slice of fresh bread.

CLARIFIED BUTTER

To clarify butter, heat it in a saucepan over low heat. As it warms, most of the water evaporates and the milk solids separate and sink to the bottom. Skim off any foam on the top and carefully pour off the melted fat without disturbing the milk solids at the bottom. The pure fat can be used with high heat—thereby avoiding the problem of browning, or burning, the milk solids, which can impart a bitter taste to cooked foods.

Soups and Stocks

Salmon House Seafood Chowder

Everyone at the Salmon House eats a bowl of chowder every day. The chowder is rich and thick with a mixture of fish and seafood.

6 cups	salmon stock (see page 56)	1.5 L
4 Tbsp.	butter	60 mL
1/2 cup	diced onions	120 mL
1/4 cup	diced celery	60 mL
1/4 cup	diced peeled carrots	60 mL
4 Tbsp.	all-purpose flour	60 mL
2 Tbsp.	tomato paste	30 mL
1/2 cup	canned plum tomatoes	120 mL
1/2 cup	tomato juice	120 mL
3/4 cup	Clamato juice	180 mL
1 Tbsp.	chopped fresh dill	15 mL
1 Tbsp.	chopped fresh basil	15 mL
1 Tbsp.	chopped fresh thyme	15 mL
3 Tbsp.	diced green onion	45 mL
1 tsp.	Worcestershire sauce	5 mL
1 tsp.	soy sauce	5 mL
1 tsp.	black pepper	5 mL
1 tsp.	salt	5 mL
1 Tbsp.	sugar	15 mL
1/2 tsp.	hot pepper sauce	2.5 mL
2 Tbsp.	zucchini, roasted (see page 143) and chopped	30 mL
2 Tbsp.	sweet red pepper, roasted (see page 143) and chopped	30 mL
5 oz.	shrimp	140 g
8 oz.	salmon	225 g
8 oz.	mixed fish, such as snapper, swordfish, halibut, etc.	225 g

Bring the stock to a simmer in a saucepan.

Melt the butter in a large stockpot over medium heat. Add the diced onion, celery and carrots and sauté for 10 minutes. Add the flour, mix well and cook for another 5 minutes. Add the tomato paste and cook for another 5 minutes. Stir in the hot fish stock until the mixture is smooth, stirring constantly to prevent lumping.

Add tomatoes, tomato and Clamato juice, dill, basil, thyme, green onion, Worcestershire and soy sauce, pepper, salt, sugar, hot pepper sauce, zucchini and red pepper. Bring to a simmer and cook for 30 minutes. Grill fish for 3 to 5 minutes a side, depending on thickness of fish. Add the shrimp, salmon and other fish and simmer another 10 minutes.

GRILLING WITH WOOD CHIPS

Wood chips can be used if you want to add a smoke flavor. Add 1 to 2 cups (240 to 475 mL) of presoaked wood chips to the coals just before you start to cook, and again when you replenish the coals. Wood chops and chunks are available at gourmet shops, hardware stores and supermarkets. Look for hardwood chunks, such as hickory, oak, cherry, alder or mesquite. Soak the chips in a bowl of cold water, enough to cover them, for 1 hour.

Salmon House Hot Pot

I have used grapeseed oil in this recipe because it is a very neutral oil and does not add any flavor. You can substitute any oil, keeping in mind that oils do add flavor.

1/4 cup	grapeseed oil	60 mL
1	onion, cut into 1-inch (2.5-cm) triangles	1
1	carrot, peeled and thinly sliced on the diagonal	1
1	rib celery, thinly sliced on the diagonal	1
1/2 lb.	chorizo, cooked and sliced into 8 pieces	225 g
12	clams, purged (see page 39)	12
12	mussels, washed and beards removed (see page 41)	12
8	tiger prawns, butterflied (see page 49)	8
4	2-oz. (57-g) boneless skinless salmon fillets	4
12	snow peas	12
1	head bok choy, cut into quarters	1
1	small jalapeño pepper, stem and seeds removed, finely diced	1
1/4 cup	chopped green onion	60 mL
2 Tbsp.	chopped cilantro	30 mL
1/4 cup	ginger wine	60 mL
4 cups	salmon stock (see page 56)	1 L
	salt and black pepper to taste	

Heat the oil in a pot over medium heat and add the onion, carrot, celery and chorizo. Cook for 5 minutes and add the clams, mussels and prawns. Cook about 2 minutes and add everything except for the salt and pepper. Cover and simmer for 5 minutes. Season with salt and pepper. Divide the seafood evenly among 4 bowls and pour the broth over it.

Almond-Crusted Chicken
with Tandoori-Fried Onions and
Mango Mustard Purée (page 95)

Moon with Frog Crest
by Vern Ezertza

Salmon House on the Hill dining room

Garlic-Crusted Ling Cod with Prawns
in Red Pepper Sauce (page 116)

Oyster and Indian Popcorn Bisque

I am told some people call dried seaweed Indian popcorn. When done right it is light, crunchy and salty. When the seaweed is added to a warm liquid it returns to its spinach-like form and adds a salty taste of the ocean to whatever you are preparing.

8	small oysters, 2 inches (5 cm) long when shucked	8
4 cups	water	1 L
1 Tbsp.	butter	15 mL
2 Tbsp.	minced onion	30 mL
1 Tbsp.	minced celery	15 mL
2 cups	whipping cream	475 mL
1 tsp.	lemon juice	5 mL
2 Tbsp.	chopped fresh dill	30 mL
1 Tbsp.	chopped fresh parsley	15 mL
1/2 tsp.	grated fresh nutmeg	2.5 mL
1/2 cup	dried seaweed	120 mL
	salt and black pepper to taste	

Place the oysters and water in a pot and bring to a boil. Reduce the heat and simmer for 2 minutes. Remove the oysters, pat them dry and cut them into quarters. Continue boiling the water until it is reduced by half. Skim any froth off the top. Melt the butter in a saucepan over medium heat and sauté the onion and celery until transparent, about 5 minutes. Strain in the oyster stock and add the cream. Bring it to a boil, then reduce to a simmer. Add the oysters, lemon juice, dill, parsley, nutmeg, seaweed, salt and pepper. Simmer for 5 minutes and serve with bread.

BUTTERFLYING PRAWNS

To butterfly prawns, first remove the greyish vein from the back with the tip of a sharp knife. Once the vein has been removed, make a deeper lengthwise cut in the flesh, almost entirely through it. Cut almost to the tail. (This can be done with or without the shell on.) Then spread the two halves apart so they lie flat in a butterfly shape.

SOUPS AND STOCKS

Garlic and Onion Soup

This garlicky soup goes well with a large crouton topped with blue cheese.

1/2 cup	olive oil	120 mL
3 1/2 cups	sliced onion	840 mL
1/3 cup	sliced garlic	80 mL
2/3 cup	roasted chopped elephant garlic (see page 13)	160 mL
6 cups	chicken stock (see page 57)	1.5 L
1/2 cup	chopped green onions	120 mL
1 Tbsp.	salt	15 mL
2 Tbsp.	black pepper	30 mL
2 Tbsp.	Worcestershire sauce	30 mL
1/3 cup	red wine	80 mL

Heat the oil in a heavy pot over medium heat. Sauté the onions until they brown and start to caramelize, about 5 minutes. Add the sliced and roasted garlic and cook for another 10 minutes over medium heat, stirring continually to prevent burning. Add the stock and bring to a boil. Add the green onions, salt, pepper, Worcestershire sauce and red wine. Simmer for 30 to 40 minutes.

Tomato, Potato and Onion Soup

An old adage says that only the true at heart can make good soup, and this is a great soup with which to test yourself.

1/4 cup	olive oil	60 mL
1 cup	sliced onion	240 mL
4	tomatoes, quartered, and seeds removed	4
4 Tbsp.	tomato paste	60 mL
1 Tbsp.	roasted garlic (see page 13)	15 mL
6 cups	vegetable or chicken stock (see page 58 or 57)	1.5 L
1/2 lb.	russet potatoes, peeled and quartered	225 g
1	bouquet garni of thyme, basil and parsley	1
1 tsp.	salt	5 mL
1 tsp.	black pepper	5 mL
1/2 cup	cream	120 mL

Heat the oil over medium heat, add the onions and sweat until transparent, about 10 minutes. Turn up the heat and add the tomatoes, tomato paste and garlic. Sauté for 5 to 10 minutes. Deglaze the pan with a little stock and add the potatoes and herbs. Add the remaining stock and bring to a boil. Reduce the heat to a simmer and cook for 45 minutes.

Remove the herbs. Working in batches, blend the soup in a food processor until it is smooth. Place the soup back in the pot and add the salt, pepper and cream. Simmer for 10 minutes.

BOUQUET GARNI

A bouquet garni is a mixture of herbs wrapped in cheesecloth and tied with a piece of string. It is placed in a stock or soup to add flavor without leaving the herbs in the soup. After the soup is done, the package of herbs is removed.

SOUPS AND STOCKS

51

Zucchini and Garlic Soup

Zucchini is a juicy vegetable that absorbs flavor—in this case, garlic.

6 cups	chicken or vegetable stock (see page 57 or 58)	1.5 L
4 cups	diced zucchini	1 L
4 Tbsp.	butter	60 mL
1/2 cup	minced onion	120 mL
1/4 cup	roasted garlic (see page 13)	60 mL
4 Tbsp.	flour	60 mL
1 tsp.	salt	5 mL
1 tsp.	black pepper	5 mL
1/2 cup	whipping cream	120 mL
1/2 cup	croutons	120 mL
1 Tbsp.	chopped fresh chives	15 mL

Bring the stock to a boil, add the zucchini and cook for 5 minutes. Remove the zucchini with a slotted spoon. Keep the stock hot.

Melt the butter in a saucepan over medium heat, add the onion and garlic and sauté in butter for 2 minutes. Do not let it brown. Add the flour and cook to a golden yellow, about 2 to 5 minutes.

Add 1/3 of the hot stock and whisk until smooth. Remove it from the heat if it splatters. Add another 1/3 of the stock and whisk until smooth over medium-high heat. Once the soup returns to a boil, add the last 1/3 of the stock. Whisk until it's smooth and returns to a boil. Reduce to a simmer and add half of the zucchini. Simmer for 30 minutes.

Blend the soup to a purée in a food processor, and return it to the pot. Add the remaining zucchini, salt, pepper and cream. Simmer for 5 minutes. Top with a few croutons and chopped chives just before serving.

Mushroom Dill Cream Soup

There are many types of mushrooms available and they all have different flavors and even different colors. Cultivated white mushrooms and brown or yellow oyster mushrooms are the ones I like to use.

2 Tbsp.	butter	30 mL
2 Tbsp.	olive oil	30 mL
2 cups	minced mushrooms	475 mL
1/2 cup	minced onion	120 mL
1 Tbsp.	roasted garlic (see page 13)	15 mL
4 Tbsp.	flour	60 mL
2 cups	water, vegetable or chicken stock (see page 58 or 57)	475 mL
1/4 cup	chopped fresh dill	60 mL
1 tsp.	salt	5 mL
1 tsp.	black pepper	5 mL
1 cup	whipping cream	240 mL

Heat the butter and oil in a heavy pot over medium-high heat. Sauté the mushrooms, onion and garlic for about 5 minutes, stirring constantly so nothing sticks. Reduce the heat to medium, and stir in the flour.

Add the stock 1/3 at a time, whisking until smooth and returning to a boil before adding the next 1/3. Add the dill, salt and pepper. Simmer for 30 minutes. Add the cream and heat through before serving.

Creamy Spinach and Pernod
with Puff Pastry and Garlic Soup

The presentation makes this a very elegant soup. When the pastry is broken, the aroma of the Pernod is a real bonus.

$1/4$ cup	minced onion	60 mL
$1/2$ tsp.	minced garlic	2.5 mL
2 Tbsp.	butter	30 mL
2 Tbsp.	flour	30 mL
2 cups	vegetable or chicken stock (see page 58 or 57)	475 mL
4 cups	washed, chopped, packed spinach	1 L
1 tsp.	salt	5 mL
1 tsp.	black pepper	5 mL
2 cups	whipping cream	475 mL
$1/4$ cup	Pernod, or pastis	60 mL
2 Tbsp.	chopped fresh chives	30 mL
4	5-inch (12.5-cm) circles of puff pastry	4
1	egg, beaten	1
2	cloves garlic, thinly sliced	2
1 tsp.	cracked black pepper	5 mL

Heat the butter in a saucepan over medium heat. Add the onion and garlic and sauté until golden brown. Stir in the flour and cook for 2 minutes. Stir in 1 cup (240 mL) of the stock. Add half the spinach, and the salt and pepper and bring to a boil. Add the rest of the stock, remove from the heat and process in a blender until it is smooth. (Be careful that the top of the blender is well secured. I cover the top with a thick cloth and hold it down while puréeing.)

Return the mixture to the pot and add the cream. Bring back to a boil, then reduce to a simmer, add the rest of the spinach and the pernod. Simmer for 10 minutes and remove from the heat.

Preheat the oven to 400°F (200°C).

Fill 4 4-inch (10-cm) heatproof bowls to ³/₄ inch (1.9 cm) from the top. Make sure the rim and outside of the bowl is wiped clean. Brush each pastry round with egg wash and cover the top of the soup bowl, pressing the pastry firmly onto the side of the bowl. Brush the top of each pastry with egg wash and stick 2 to 3 slices of garlic on the pastry. Sprinkle a little cracked black pepper on top.

Place the bowls well apart on a baking sheet and bake for 10 minutes. Reduce the heat to 375°F (190°C) and bake for 5 minutes more. The pastry should be golden and form a dome shape. Warn your guests to be careful when they cut open the pastry—the steam is hot.

ABOUT PASTRY

Adding fat and eggs to pastry gives it a lighter consistency. The simpler the pastry (that is, the less fat it contains), the more complex the construction that can be made with it. A "short" crust contains more fat and less liquid, which creates a crumbly, difficult-to-handle but delicious pastry. Note that flour must be fresh and smell pleasantly of wheat. Do not overmix the dough and do not use too much flour on the table when you're rolling it out. Both will create a less tender crust.

Salmon Stock

Salmon stock is strong fish stock. And just as the fish of the Mediterranean flavor the classical bouillabaisse, salmon gives our West Coast stocks a unique flavor. If you are using fish heads, be sure to have the gills removed. Any fish can be used.

1 lb.	salmon bones, washed (see page 83)	455 g
1 Tbsp.	vegetable oil	15 mL
8 cups	cold water	2 L
1 cup	diced onion	240 mL
1/4 cup	diced carrot	60 mL
1/4 cup	diced celery	60 mL
1/4 cup	chopped leeks	60 mL
1	bay leaf	1
1 Tbsp.	chopped fresh basil	15 mL
1 Tbsp.	chopped fresh thyme	15 mL
1/4 cup	chopped green onion	60 mL
1 Tbsp.	salt	15 mL
1 Tbsp.	cracked black pepper	15 mL
1/4 cup	white wine	60 mL

Toss the bones in the oil. Grill for 10 to 15 minutes over a medium-high heat or roast in the oven for 1 hour at 325°F (165°C).

Put the bones in a pot large enough to hold the stock. Add the water and all other ingredients. Bring to a simmer and cook for an hour. (Since the bones are small, a long period of cooking is not needed.) Strain the stock through a fine mesh strainer or cheesecloth and chill over ice. Refrigerate for up to 4 days, or freeze for later use.

Chicken Stock

Chicken stock can be made from raw bones, roasted bones, leftover carcasses or whole boiling fowl. It is a base for soups, sauces, risottos and can even be used to simmer vegetables in. The key to a clear stock is to skim the fat and foam from the surface and cook at a very low simmer. Enjoy the aroma, especially on a rainy day.

1 lb.	chicken bones, washed (see page 83)	455 g
2 Tbsp.	vegetable oil	30 mL
8 cups	water	2 L
1/2 cup	diced onion	120 mL
1/4 cup	diced carrot	60 mL
1/4 cup	diced celery	60 mL
1/4 cup	chopped leeks	60 mL
1	bay leaf	1
1 Tbsp.	chopped fresh basil	15 mL
1 Tbsp.	chopped fresh thyme	15 mL
1/4 cup	chopped green onion	60 mL
1 Tbsp.	salt	15 mL
1 Tbsp.	cracked black pepper	15 mL
5	whole cloves	5
1	stalk lemon grass, chopped	1
1	lemon, juice only	1

Preheat the oven to 350°F (175°C). Toss the bones in the vegetable oil. Roast in the oven for 2 hours, turning the bones to make sure both sides get golden brown.

Place the roasted bones and all other ingredients in a pot and bring to a simmer. This stock should cook for at least 6 hours. Strain and refrigerate or freeze.

SOUPS AND STOCKS

Vegetable Stock

This stock changes with the vegetables you use or your choice of herbs. Cilantro, rosemary and sage are very strong—unless you want that flavor, don't add them. And avoid strong-flavored vegetables like asparagus, broccoli, cauliflower, turnips and parsnips unless you want the predominant flavor of that vegetable.

5 lbs.	assorted vegetables	2.25 kg
2 Tbsp.	chopped fresh thyme	30 mL
2 Tbsp.	chopped fresh basil	30 mL
2 Tbsp.	chopped fresh chives	30 mL
2 Tbsp.	chopped fresh dill	30 mL
4	bay leaves	4
2 Tbsp.	cracked black pepper	30 mL
1 tsp.	salt	5 mL
8 cups	water	2 L

Put everything in a pot and simmer for 1 hour. Strain. For a richer stock, you can roast the vegetables before simmering. Toss them in a little oil and roast at 350°F (175°C) for 30 minutes.

Strain and cool down over ice. Keep refrigerated for up to 4 days, or freeze for later use.

Brown Stock

Brown stock is considered the backbone of classic French cuisine, and well-made brown stock is essential to many types of meat dishes. The bones are roasted to give a richer, darker stock. Veal bones are used because the bones are from a younger animal and therefore produce a milder, more neutral stock. Stock made with beef bones is fine for all beef dishes.

4 lbs.	veal bones, preferably knuckle and shank (see page 83)	1.8 kg
1 Tbsp.	oil	15 mL
1/4 cup	tomato paste	60 mL
1 cup	chopped carrots	240 mL
1 cup	chopped celery	240 mL
1 1/2 cups	chopped onion	360 mL
1 cup	chopped leeks	240 mL
10 cups	cold water	2.4 L
2	sprigs rosemary	2
2	sprigs thyme	2
4	bay leaves	4
1	head garlic, halved	1
2–4 Tbsp.	whole black pepper, cracked	30–60 mL
2 Tbsp.	minced fresh ginger	30 mL
2 Tbsp.	Worcestershire sauce	30 mL

Preheat the oven to 350°F (175°C).

Toss the bones with the oil, place them in a baking pan and roast for 1 1/2 hours. After 1/2 hour, turn the bones over. Spread the tomato paste over the bones and add the carrots, celery and onion. Add the leeks 15 minutes later. Stir the leeks with the tomato paste and oil to keep them moist and prevent burning. Return the pan to the oven and roast for 1 more hour. A dark, golden-brown roast is what you want. The tomato paste on exposed bones should blacken a little.

Scrape the bones and vegetables into a stockpot. Cover with the water and bring to a boil. Turn down to a simmer and skim off any fat or foam that rises to the surface. Add the rosemary, thyme, bay leaves, garlic, pepper, ginger and Worcestershire sauce. Simmer for 10 to 12 hours. Strain the stock into a clean pot and chill over ice. Refrigerate up to 4 days, or freeze for later use.

SOUPS AND STOCKS

Salads

Mesclun Greens and Beet Chips

This would work well using any greens from butter lettuce to endive. Add a few chopped chives, cucumber slices and tomatoes if you want.

FOR THE VINAIGRETTE:

1/4 cup	raspberry vinegar	60 mL
3 Tbsp.	vegetable oil	45 mL
1/4 cup	olive oil	60 mL
1 Tbsp.	minced red onion	15 mL
2 tsp.	chopped fresh dill	10 mL
2 tsp.	grenadine	10 mL
2 tsp.	sugar	10 mL
	pinch salt and black pepper	

Place everything in a bowl and whisk for 2 minutes until combined.

FOR THE DRESSING:

1/2 cup	plain yogurt	120 mL
1 Tbsp.	minced fresh dill	15 mL
1 Tbsp.	lime juice	15 mL
1 Tbsp.	lime zest	15 mL
1 Tbsp.	orange juice concentrate	15 mL
1 Tbsp.	liquid honey	15 mL
	pinch minced garlic	
	salt and black pepper to taste	

Combine everything in a bowl and mix well. Cover and refrigerate. Use leftovers as a vegetable dip.

FOR THE BEET CHIPS:

1	beet, 3 inches (7.5 cm) in diameter	1
3 Tbsp.	cornstarch	45 mL
4 cups	vegetable oil	1 L

Peel the beet and cut it into slices about $^1/_{16}$ inch (1 mm) thick. Heat the oil to 350°F (175°C) in a deep, heavy pot. Do not fill it more than $^1/_2$ full. Dust the beet slices with cornstarch and fry them in the oil, a few at a time, until crisp. They should cook in a single layer. When the bubbles have disappeared from the beet slices, remove and drain on paper towel.

TO MAKE THE SALAD:

4 cups	mesclun greens	1 L
$^1/_2$ cup	vinaigrette	120 mL
1 cup	beet chips	240 mL
$^1/_2$ cup	dressing	120 mL

In a mixing bowl toss the greens with the vinaigrette. Divide equally between 4 plates. Scatter the beet chips over the greens and drizzle the dressing over the salads.

Fresh Fruit Salad
with Black Pepper Vanilla Bean Vinaigrette

With all of the fresh berries and fruit of summer, you can have a new adventure every time you serve this salad. You can buy vanilla beans at any specialty store.

2 Tbsp.	rice vinegar	30 mL
2 Tbsp.	lime juice	30 mL
1 Tbsp.	coarsely ground black pepper	15 mL
1	vanilla bean, split lengthwise and seeds scraped out	1
1/2 cup	olive oil	120 mL
	pinch salt	
3 cups	mesclun greens	720 mL
1/2 cup	strawberries, hulled and cut in half	120 mL
1/2 cup	raspberries	120 mL
1/2 cup	blueberries	120 mL
2 Tbsp.	chopped fresh chives	30 mL

To make the vinaigrette, combine the vinegar, lime juice, black pepper and vanilla bean seeds in a bowl. Slowly whisk in the oil and salt. In another bowl, combine the greens and berries. Pour 3/4 of the vinaigrette over the salad and toss. Divide evenly among 4 plates and top with the chives. Pour the rest of the vinaigrette around each plate.

Hot Scallop Salad
with Butter Lettuce, Mustard, Tarragon and Sherry

Scallops the size of hockey pucks are available, but for this recipe I use ones about 1-inch (2.5-cm) across. I like to cook scallops to medium doneness, but you have to watch that they don't overcook and become rubbery.

3 Tbsp.	olive oil	45 mL
16	scallops, tendon removed (see page 123)	16
1/4 cup	minced onion	60 mL
1 tsp.	minced garlic	5 mL
4 tsp.	Dijon mustard	20 mL
4 tsp.	grainy mustard	20 mL
4 tsp.	chopped fresh tarragon	20 mL
1/2 cup	dry sherry	120 mL
1/2 cup	whipping cream	120 mL
1/2 tsp.	salt	2.5 mL
1 tsp.	black pepper	5 mL
1	head butter lettuce	1

Heat the oil in a sauté pan over medium heat. Add the scallops and cook for about 1 minute on each side. Add the onion, garlic, mustards and tarragon. Toss and add the sherry. When the mixture comes to a boil, add the cream, salt and pepper. Cook until it's reduced by half.

Cut the lettuce in quarters and place each piece in the middle of a plate. Pour the scallop mixture over top and serve immediately.

Cajun Fried Green Tomatoes
with Crispy Onions and Stilton Buttermilk Dressing

Thick slices of hard-as-a-rock green tomatoes are absolutely incredible when fried. I use English Stilton because of its crumbly, mixable quality. For this salad you can use your favorite cheese, if blue is not your first choice.

1/2 cup	flour	120 mL
1 tsp.	salt	5 mL
	pinch garlic powder	
	pinch black pepper	
1/4 cup	very thinly sliced onions	60 mL
4 cups	vegetable oil for frying	1 L
12	3/4-inch (1.9-cm) slices of tomato, approximately 3 inches (7.5 cm) in diameter	12
1/2 cup	Cajun Spice	120 mL
1/4 cup	olive oil	60 mL
1 cup	Stilton Buttermilk Dressing	240 mL

Combine the flour, salt, garlic powder and pepper in a bowl. Toss the sliced onions in the flour mixture. Heat the 4 cups (950 mL) oil in a small pan until it is 350°F (175°C). Shake off any loose flour and fry the onions in the oil until crisp, about 5 minutes. Drain on a paper towel. Toss the tomatoes in the Cajun spice. Heat the olive oil in a frying pan to medium heat and fry the tomatoes for 2 to 3 minutes on each side. The tomatoes should be crisp, not mushy or soft (it would still taste good, but it's not the effect we are trying for). Pour 1/4 cup (60 mL) of dressing on each plate, place 3 slices of tomato over the dressing and top with the fried onion.

Cajun Spice

		MAKES 1 CUP (240 ML)
1/4 cup	Mexican chili powder	60 mL
2 Tbsp.	cayenne pepper	30 mL
2 Tbsp.	ground cumin	30 mL
2 Tbsp.	ground coriander	30 mL
2 Tbsp.	lemon pepper	30 mL
2 Tbsp.	salt	30 mL
1 Tbsp.	paprika	15 mL
2 Tbsp.	garlic powder	30 mL
1/4 cup	flour	60 mL
1 Tbsp.	dried oregano	15 mL
1 Tbsp.	dried thyme	15 mL

Mix everything together. This mixture will keep in an airtight container for months. You can make the mix hotter or milder by omitting the flour or adding more.

Stilton Buttermilk Dressing

		MAKES 1 1/2 CUPS (360 ML)
6 oz.	Stilton cheese, grated	170 g
1 tsp.	Dijon mustard	5 mL
1 tsp.	lemon juice	5 mL
1 tsp.	lemon zest	5 mL
	pinch salt	
1/2 Tbsp.	lemon pepper	7.5 mL
1 cup	buttermilk	240 mL

In a mixing bowl combine the cheese, mustard, lemon juice and zest, salt and lemon pepper. Whisk in the buttermilk.

This can be refrigerated for up to a week. Leftovers can be used as a vegetable dip or salad dressing.

Chili-Cumin Dusted Scallops
with Tomatoes and Blue Cheese Toasts

Mexican chili powder and cumin is a very hot combination, so beware. Gorgonzola is a rich blue cheese from the Lombardy region of Italy. You can substitute any blue cheese you like.

4 Tbsp.	Mexican chili powder	60 mL
1 Tbsp.	ground cumin	15 mL
1/2 tsp.	salt	2.5 mL
1 tsp.	black pepper	5 mL
1/2	head iceberg lettuce, cut into 4 wedges	1/2
1/4 cup	olive oil	60 mL
4 oz.	Gorgonzola cheese	113 g
12	slices baguette	12
16	scallops, 20/30 count (see page 119)	16
1/2 cup	minced onion	120 mL
1/2 tsp.	minced garlic	2.5 mL
1 cup	diced and seeded tomato	240 mL
1/2 cup	white wine	120 mL
4 Tbsp.	chopped fresh chives	60 mL

Preheat the oven to 400°F (200°C).

Combine the chili powder, cumin, salt and pepper together. Dust the wedges of lettuce with a little of the spice mix. Heat a little of the oil in a frying pan over high heat, and fry the lettuce wedges until both sides are browned. It should not take more than 1 minute per side. Set out 4 plates and place a lettuce wedge on each one.

Evenly spread the cheese over the bread, place on a baking sheet and bake for 5 minutes.

Toss the scallops in the remaining spice mix and shake off the excess. Heat the rest of the oil in a sauté pan over medium-high heat and sauté the scallops for about 2 minutes. Add the onion, garlic and tomato. Cook for 2 minutes and add the wine and chives. Spoon the scallops over the lettuce and place 3 cheese toasts around each plate.

SALADS

Canned Salmon Salad
with Shaved Fennel and Beet Crème Fraîche

When choosing fennel, always look for the round bulb (the female plant) versus the elongated flat bulb (male plant). Female plants are more flavorful and are never woody or tough. Any type of canned salmon is suitable in this recipe.

2	6-oz. (170-g) cans salmon	2
1/2 cup	chopped green onions	120 mL
1/2 cup	diced sweet red pepper	120 mL
2 Tbsp.	lemon juice	30 mL
1/2 tsp.	salt	2.5 mL
1 tsp.	black pepper	5 mL
2 cups	thinly shaved fennel bulb	475 mL
2 Tbsp.	raspberry vinegar	30 mL
2 Tbsp.	olive oil	30 mL
	pinch salt and black pepper	
1 cup	pickled beets	240 mL
1/2 cup	crème fraîche (see page 73)	120 mL
2 Tbsp.	chopped fresh chives	30 mL

Place the salmon in a mixing bowl. (Removing the skin and bones is optional.) Break it up slightly with a fork and mix in the green onion, red pepper, lemon juice, salt and pepper. Toss the shaved fennel with the vinegar and oil. Season with salt and pepper. Divide the beets in half. Place one-half in a blender with the crème fraîche and purée.

To assemble the salad, arrange the fennel on 4 plates and top with the salmon mix. Pour the crème fraîche purée over and top with the remaining beets and the chives.

SALADS

69

Salmon House Caesar Salad

Caesar salad with all its different styles—even grilling the lettuce—has outlived all other salads in popularity. Here is our version.

1	egg	1
2 Tbsp.	grated Parmesan cheese	30 mL
1 Tbsp.	minced garlic	15 mL
4	anchovies in oil	4
1 tsp.	salt	5 mL
1/2 tsp.	freshly ground black pepper	2.5 mL
1 1/2 Tbsp.	capers and juice, puréed	22.5 mL
1 1/2 Tbsp.	Dijon mustard	22.5 mL
3 Tbsp.	sour cream	45 mL
	dash hot pepper sauce	
1 tsp.	Worcestershire sauce	5 mL
1 tsp.	soy sauce	5 mL
1 1/2 cups	vegetable oil	360 mL
3/4 cup	olive oil	180 mL
1 1/2 Tbsp.	fresh lemon juice	22.5 mL
1 1/2 Tbsp.	red wine vinegar	22.5 mL
6 cups	romaine lettuce	1.5 L
1/2 cup	grated Parmesan cheese	120 mL
1 1/2 cups	croutons	360 mL
4	lemon wedges	4

Place the egg, 2 Tbsp. (30 mL) Parmesan cheese, garlic, anchovies and oil, salt, pepper, capers, mustard, sour cream, hot pepper sauce, Worcestershire sauce and soy sauce in a mixing bowl and stir together. Mix the oils together. Combine the lemon juice and vinegar. Alternately add the oil and vinegar mixture until the dressing is thick.

Wash and soak the lettuce for 7 minutes in ice water to crisp it up. Dry and cut it into bite-size pieces. There are those who insist that tearing the lettuce is the only way, but if you are going to eat your romaine that day, cutting it with a knife is fine.

In a mixing bowl combine the lettuce, $^1/4$ cup (60 mL) of the cheese and $^1/2$ the dressing. Mix well and divide between 4 plates. Top with the croutons and the rest of the cheese. Place a wedge of lemon on the side of each plate. The remainder of the dressing can be used as a vegetable dip or as a replacement for mayonnaise on sandwiches. It will keep refrigerated for up to 4 days.

Smoked Salmon
with Asparagus and Honeydew Purée

This is a good basic recipe that can be altered by changing the purée or even substituting another vegetable for the asparagus.

16	spears asparagus	16
16	slices smoked salmon	16
1	honeydew melon, peeled, seeds removed, diced	1

To blanch the asparagus, bring 8 cups (2 L) of salted water to a boil. Add the asparagus and cook for 1 minute. Remove from the water and cool down in iced water. Drain and pat dry. Wrap each spear of asparagus with a slice of smoked salmon.

Place the honeydew in a blender and liquefy. Pour about $^1/4$ cup (60 mL) of the purée on each of 4 plates, and place 4 asparagus spears over the purée. Serve chilled. A few chopped chives sprinkled on top is a nice touch.

SALADS

71

Baked Camembert
with Sun-Dried Berry Vinaigrette

Cheese and nuts make a winning combination. The berry vinaigrette is a tart accent and moistens the salad. Use more if you like, or pass it on the side.

FOR THE VINAIGRETTE:

2 Tbsp.	sun-dried cranberries	30 mL
2 Tbsp.	sun-dried blueberries	30 mL
2 Tbsp.	sun-dried raspberries	30 mL
2 Tbsp.	sun-dried cherries	30 mL
1/3 cup	port	80 mL
1/3 cup	water	80 mL
2 tsp.	honey	10 mL
	pinch salt and cracked black pepper	
1 tsp.	lemon zest	5 mL
1 tsp.	lemon juice	5 mL
2 tsp.	balsamic vinegar	10 mL
3 Tbsp.	olive oil	45 mL
1 tsp.	chopped fresh basil	5 mL
1 tsp.	chopped fresh thyme	5 mL
1 tsp.	chopped fresh chives	5 mL

Place the sun-dried berries in a bowl. Pour the port and water over them and cover with plastic wrap. Place over a pot of simmering water for 1/2 hour. Most of the liquid should be absorbed. Stir in the rest of the ingredients and refrigerate.

TO ASSEMBLE THE SALAD:

4	7-oz. (200-g) Camembert rounds, 3 inches (7.5 cm) in diameter	4
4 tsp.	sambal oelek	20 mL
1/4 cup	cane sugar	60 mL
1/2 cup	pine nuts, toasted	120 mL
1 cup	mesclun greens	240 mL

Preheat the oven to 400°F (200°C).

Slice the rind off the top of the cheese rounds. Spread 1 tsp. (5 mL) of sambal oelek over each. Sprinkle each with 1 Tbsp. (15 mL) sugar and 2 Tbsp. (30 mL) pine nuts. Bake for 5 minutes, or until the cheese starts to bubble. Toss the greens in the vinaigrette and divide among 4 plates. Place the cheese on the greens and serve immediately.

CRÈME FRAÎCHE

To make crème fraîche, mix together 1/3 cup (80 mL) buttermilk with 1/2 cup (120 mL) sour cream and 2 cups (475 mL) whipping cream. Cover with plastic wrap and let sit at room temperature for 24 hours, then refrigerate. It will keep in the refrigerator for up to 1 week.

SALADS

Grilled Vegetables
with Goat Cheese and Raspberry-Rosemary Vinaigrette

Vegetables contain no fat, so the marinade provides moisture and prevents them from sticking to the grill or pan. Naturally occurring sugars in the vegetables become caramelized when grilled or baked.

FOR THE GRILLED VEGETABLES:

2	carrots	2
1	zucchini	1
1	red onion	1
1	large sweet red pepper	1
8	spears asparagus	8
1	bulb fennel, about 4 inches (10 cm) long	1
2 Tbsp.	chopped fresh basil	30 mL
2 Tbsp.	chopped fresh thyme	30 mL
2 Tbsp.	chopped fresh rosemary	30 mL
2 Tbsp.	chopped fresh dill	30 mL
1 Tbsp.	minced garlic	15 mL
1 tsp.	salt	5 mL
1 Tbsp.	black pepper	15 mL
1 cup	olive oil	240 mL

Peel the carrots and slice them on the diagonal into pieces about $1/4$ inch (.6 cm) thick and 3 inches (7.5 cm) long. Peel strips from the zucchini, leaving an unpeeled portion between each strip to give a nice green and white striped effect. Cut the zucchini on the diagonal into pieces about $1/3$ inch (.8 cm) thick by 3 inches (7.5 cm) long. Peel the onion and cut it into eighths, making sure that each piece is held together by a bit of the core. Remove the seeds and stem of the red pepper, and cut it into eighths. Trim or shave off the woody stems of the asparagus. Trim the root end of the fennel and cut it into eighths, making sure the core holds each piece together.

Mix the remaining ingredients in a large bowl. Add the vegetables and toss to coat them. Cover and let sit overnight in the refrigerator.

Preheat the grill to medium or the oven to 350°F (175°C). (If you're roasting the vegetables, add the asparagus and zucchini during until the last 10 minutes of cooking.) Roast for 30 to 40 minutes, stirring every 10 minutes or so. If grilling, cook for 5 minutes; the vegetables should still be firm. Remove from the oven or grill and cool in the marinade.

FOR THE VINAIGRETTE:

1/4 cup	raspberry vinegar	60 mL
2 tsp.	minced onion	10 mL
1 Tbsp.	honey	15 mL
1/2 tsp.	salt	2.5 mL
1 tsp.	black pepper	5 mL
2 tsp.	chopped fresh rosemary	10 mL
2 tsp.	chopped fresh chives	10 mL
1/4 cup	olive oil	60 mL
1/2 cup	rosemary oil	120 mL

Mix all the ingredients except the oils in a blender. Combine the oils and slowly add them while blending on medium speed.

The vinaigrette can be refrigerated for up to a week. Leftovers can be used on salads.

TO ASSEMBLE THE SALAD:

4	2-oz. (57-g) goat cheese medallions	4
1/2 cup	raspberry-rosemary vinaigrette	120 mL
1/2 cup	raspberries	120 mL
2 Tbsp.	chopped fresh chives	30 mL
4	sprigs rosemary	4

Drain the vegetables from the marinade. Then toss the vegetables in the vinaigrette and divide among 4 plates. Top with a goat cheese medallion and garnish each with raspberries, chives and a sprig of rosemary.

Prosciutto, Melon and Mesclun Salad
with Tangy Grape Relish

Here is a classic dish rolled up to give it some height. The grape relish provides little bursts of flavor and texture.

FOR THE VINAIGRETTE:

2 Tbsp.	minced onion	30 mL
1 Tbsp.	lemon juice	15 mL
1 Tbsp.	lime juice	15 mL
	pinch salt and black pepper	
6 Tbsp.	olive oil	90 mL

Mix the onion, lemon juice, lime juice, salt and pepper. Whisk in the oil and set aside.

FOR THE RELISH:

1 cup	red seedless grapes, cut in half	240 mL
3 Tbsp.	minced onion	45 mL
2 Tbsp.	chopped fresh chives	30 mL
1 Tbsp.	finely diced sweet red pepper	15 mL
2 Tbsp.	chopped green onions	30 mL
2 Tbsp.	honey	30 mL
1 tsp.	lemon pepper	5 mL
1/2 tsp.	salt	2.5 mL
6 Tbsp.	olive oil	90 mL

Combine everything except the oil in a bowl. Slowly whisk in the oil.

TO ASSEMBLE THE SALAD:

8	slices prosciutto, 8 inches (20 cm) long, sliced thin	8
1 cup	mesclun greens	240 mL
1/4	cantaloupe, cut into 8 slices	1/4
4	sprigs fresh dill	4
4	chive blossoms with 6-inch (15-cm) stems	4

Set out 4 plates. Lay 2 pieces of prosciutto out lengthwise on a plate, overlapping them by 2 inches (5 cm). Repeat with the other 6 slices. Toss the mesclun in the vinaigrette. Divide the greens among the 4 plates, placing the greens at the bottom of the prosciutto. Place 2 slices of cantaloupe, a sprig of dill and a chive blossom on top of the greens. Roll up the prosciutto. The greens will look like a plant coming out of a pot. Stand the salad up on the plate. Place 2 to 3 Tbsp. (30 to 45 mL) of the grape relish around each salad.

The remaining relish can be served on crackers or toasted bread or as an accompaniment to meat or fish. It keeps in the refrigerator for up to a week.

Shrimp and Avocado Salad
with Fried Olives and Lemon Feta Dressing

In this salad I fry the olives in a batter, but you could toss them in a little oil and roast them in a 350°F (175°C) oven for 10 minutes instead. A good olive oil can be quite thick, especially when refrigerated. In this recipe the virgin olive oil helps the salad keep its molded shape for a while after it's taken out of the fridge.

FOR THE SALAD:

1 lb.	baby shrimp	455 g
1/2 tsp.	lemon pepper	2.5 mL
1/2 tsp.	black pepper	2.5 mL
1/4 cup	lime juice	60 mL
1/4 cup	virgin olive oil	60 mL
2	avocados	2
2 Tbsp.	lemon juice	30 mL
1 tsp.	virgin olive oil	5 mL
1/2 tsp.	salt	2.5 mL

Wash, drain and pat the shrimp dry. (It is not the shrimp that goes bad first, but its liquid.) Combine the shrimp, 1/2 the lemon pepper, black pepper, lime juice and the 4 Tbsp. (60 mL) olive oil in a bowl.

Divide the mixture into 4 and press each portion into a 1-cup (240-mL) mold. Leave a 3/4-inch (2-cm) space at the top for the avocado. Peel and seed the avocado and slice it into 1/4 x 1 1/2-inch (.6 x 4-cm) slices. Sprinkle with lemon juice, the remaining lemon pepper and 1 tsp. (5 mL) olive oil. Place the avocado evenly over the shrimp in each mold. Gently press down and refrigerate for at least 15 minutes.

FOR THE DRESSING:

2 Tbsp.	minced onion	30 mL
1 Tbsp.	lemon juice	15 mL
1/2 Tbsp.	rice wine vinegar	7.5 mL
	pinch salt and black pepper	
4 Tbsp.	crumbled feta cheese	60 mL
6 Tbsp.	olive oil	90 mL

Mix the onion, lemon juice, vinegar, salt, pepper and cheese in a bowl. Whisk in the oil and set aside.

FOR THE OLIVES:

1/4 cup	buttermilk	60 mL
1 cup	flour	240 mL
24	kalamata olives, pits removed	24
4 cups	vegetable oil	1 L

Mix the buttermilk and flour in a medium bowl. Pat the olives dry and add them to the batter. Strain. Place the oil in a large deep pot and heat it to 350°F (175°C). The pot should be no more than half full. Add the battered olives and fry for 2 minutes. Remove from the oil and drain on paper towels.

TO SERVE:

Unmold each salad using a fork or your hand to place it on a serving plate. Drizzle the dressing around each salad and top with the olives.

Meat and Poultry

Filet Mignon
with Curried Crab Claws

This is steak and crab with a little twist. Beef tenderloin can be a little dry some-times because it doesn't have very much fat, if any. Smothering the beef with the curry sauce is very tasty. We prefer snow crab because of the flavor, but any kind of crab can be used. It is delicious served on a bed of golden basmati rice.

4	6-oz. (170-g) medallions of beef tenderloin	4
1 Tbsp.	minced garlic	15 mL
1 Tbsp.	minced fresh ginger	15 mL
1 tsp.	salt	5 mL
1 tsp.	coarsely ground Szechuan peppercorns	5 mL
1/4 cup	vegetable oil	60 mL
4 Tbsp.	clarified butter (see page 44)	60 mL
1 tsp.	minced fresh ginger	5 mL
1/2 tsp.	minced garlic	2.5 mL
6 Tbsp.	minced onion	90 mL
1/4 tsp.	ground cumin	1.2 mL
1/4 tsp.	ground coriander	1.2 mL
1/4 tsp.	garam masala	1.2 mL
1/4 tsp.	ground cinnamon	1.2 mL
1/4 tsp.	powdered turmeric	1.2 mL
1 tsp.	curry powder	5 mL
3 cups	vegetable stock (see page 58)	720 mL
1/2 cup	chopped mango	120 mL
4 Tbsp.	tomato concasse (see page 99)	60 mL
4 Tbsp.	chopped green onions	60 mL
1 Tbsp.	chopped cilantro	15 mL
1 Tbsp.	chopped fresh parsley	15 mL
12	1-oz. (28-g) snow crab claws, shells removed	12
	salt and black pepper to taste	

Rub the beef with the 1 Tbsp. (15 mL) of garlic and ginger, salt and Szechuan peppercorns. Cover with the oil and refrigerate for at least an hour.

Place the clarified butter in a 12-inch (30-cm) heavy frying pan over medium heat. Add the 1 tsp. (5 mL) ginger, $1/2$ tsp. (2.5 mL) garlic, onion, cumin, coriander, garam masala, cinnamon, turmeric and curry powder, and sauté for 1 minute. Add 2 cups (475 mL) of the vegetable stock and continue cooking until it's reduced by half. Add the mango, tomato concasse, green onions, cilantro, parsley and crab claws. Add the remaining 1 cup (240 mL) vegetable stock and cook over high heat until the sauce is the consistency of light cream. Season with salt and pepper.

Heat the grill to medium-high. Cook the steaks for about 5 minutes per side for medium-rare to rare. When the steaks are done, place on plates and spoon the curried crab claws over the meat.

MAKING STOCK

When making stock, always wash the bones to get rid of the blood, which can cloud the stock and change its flavor. You can either wash the bones under cold water until the blood is gone, or cook them in boiling water for about 1 minute, then drain and rinse. Roasting the bones is the difference between a mediocre and excellent stock. Roasting darkens the bones and cooks out the gelatin, which creates a richer stock. We grill the bones over alder, which adds a smoky flavor. For fish stock, roast the bones 45 minutes to 1 hour; for chicken stock, 1 to 1 $1/2$ hours; for beef stock, 1 $1/2$ to 2 hours. All soup stocks will keep for up to 4 days in the refrigerator and all freeze well.

Grilled Beef Tenderloin
with Greek Olive Tapenade

Here is a nice alternative to serving meat with a sauce. With the tapenade and salad, it makes a light meal in itself.

FOR THE TAPENADE:

1 1/2 cups	black Greek olives, pitted and washed	360 mL
4	anchovy fillets	4
3 Tbsp.	capers	45 mL
1 tsp.	minced garlic	5 mL
1	lemon, juice only	1
1/2 tsp.	black pepper	2.5 mL
1/4 cup	olive oil	60 mL
2 Tbsp.	chopped fresh basil	30 mL

In a food processor combine the olives, anchovies, capers, garlic, lemon juice and pepper. Pulse until coarsely chopped and pour into a bowl. Stir in the olive oil and add the basil.

FOR THE ONIONS:

16	thin slices red onion	16
1	lemon, juice only	1
1/2 tsp.	black pepper	2.5 mL

Marinate the onions in lemon juice and pepper for 30 minutes.

FOR THE VINAIGRETTE:

1 Tbsp.	red wine vinegar	15 mL
1 Tbsp.	Dijon mustard	15 mL
1 Tbsp.	grainy mustard	15 mL
1/2 tsp.	salt	2.5 mL
1/2 tsp.	black pepper	2.5 mL
1/4 cup	olive oil	60 mL

Prepare the vinaigrette by combining the vinegar, mustards, salt and pepper. Gradually whisk in the oil until emulsified.

TO ASSEMBLE THE DISH:

4	6-oz. (170-g) beef tenderloin steaks	4
	salt and black pepper to taste	
4 cups	watercress, washed and trimmed	1 L
1/2 cup	trimmed and thinly sliced radishes	120 mL
2 Tbsp.	chopped green onions	30 mL
2 Tbsp.	thinly sliced fresh basil	30 mL
1/2 tsp.	black pepper	2.5 mL

Season the meat with salt and pepper. Heat the grill to medium-high and grill the steaks for about 5 minutes on each side for medium-rare.

When you are ready to serve, spread the tapenade on 4 plates. Divide the red onions over the tapenade. Place the beef in the center of the tapenade. Toss the watercress, radishes, green onions and basil with the vinaigrette and pile the salad over the beef. Sprinkle with the pepper.

ABOUT TAMARIND

Tamarind is the fruit of a tropical tree. The long brown seed pod contains a sweet-sour pulp that tastes like puréed prunes mixed with lime juice. Tamarind is used to flavor Worcestershire sauce and A-1 steak sauce. Tamarind is a staple in the Caribbean, India and Southeast Asia, and it is slowly becoming known in North America. If you live in a city with a large Hispanic or Asian population, you may be able to find fresh tamarind pods. Asian markets often sell sticky balls of peeled tamarind pulp. Watch out for the seeds and remove them. The canned pulp or paste is also available in Asian markets.

Jalapeño-Crusted New York Steaks
with Adobo Mushroom Sauce

You can make your own adobo sauce or use the sauce from a can of chipotle peppers in adobo sauce. If you like, add the chipotle peppers as well, but the heat will most definitely increase. This recipe for adobo sauce makes more than is needed for the dish. You can store the sauce in the refrigerator for a week or freeze it.

1/3 cup	olive oil	80 mL
3	sweet red peppers, seeds and stems removed, julienned	3
1/2 cup	olive oil	120 mL
2 cups	sliced shiitake or portobello mushrooms	475 mL
1 Tbsp.	minced garlic	15 mL
4 Tbsp.	Adobo Sauce	60 mL
2 Tbsp.	Worcestershire sauce	30 mL
1 cup	vegetable stock (see page 58)	240 mL
	salt and black pepper to taste	
4	9-oz. (255-g) New York steaks	4
4 Tbsp.	olive oil	60 mL
4	jalapeños, seeds and stems removed, minced	4
2 Tbsp.	chopped fresh parsley	30 mL

Heat the 1/3 cup (80 mL) olive oil over medium heat. Add the red peppers and sauté until soft, about 20 minutes. Remove from the heat and purée. Heat the 1/2 cup (120 mL) oil over medium-high heat. Add the mushrooms and sauté for 5 minutes. Add the garlic and toss once or twice. Strain off the excess oil. Add the adobo and Worcestershire sauces. Toss again and add the vegetable stock and red pepper purée. Simmer until most of the liquid is gone, about 10 minutes. Season with salt and pepper. Keep warm while you prepare the steaks.

Season the steaks with salt and pepper and brush with the 4 Tbsp. (60 mL) olive oil. Evenly press the minced jalapeño on one side of each of the steaks. Fry the steaks jalapeño side down first to sear the peppers. Carefully turn the steaks over and sear the other side. Remove the steaks and finish cooking them on the grill or under the broiler, about 3 to 5 minutes a side.

To serve, place the steaks on a plate, spoon the sauce over the steaks and sprinkle with chopped parsley.

Adobo Sauce

		MAKES 2 CUPS (475 ML)
2 cups	canned tomatoes	475 mL
6 Tbsp.	chili powder	90 mL
1	chipotle pepper	1
1 Tbsp.	honey	15 mL
3 Tbsp.	red wine vinegar	45 mL
1 tsp.	cayenne pepper	5 mL
1/4 cup	minced garlic	60 mL
1/4 cup	olive oil	60 mL

Place everything in a food processor and purée. Simmer over very low heat for 20 minutes.

GRILLING STEAK

When I grill a steak, I turn it 3 times, letting the heat touch each side twice. Some people think marking a steak is important, but I have never had a steak sent back for bad lines. Even cooking on each side, knowing the heat and watching for the juices are keys to a good steak. When the heat reaches the center of a piece of meat, the juices have nowhere else to go and they start running. I call this "medium-rare running." When the juice turns clear, we are looking at a medium steak. No juice means it is medium-well done and shortly after that it's well done.

MEAT AND POULTRY

87

Grilled New York Steak
with Black Truffle Oil, Tarragon Butter and Brown Sauce

Truffles are mushrooms that grow underground and therefore have an earthy flavor. They are usually black, but there are white ones that have a slight flavor of garlic. The oil is made from the mushroom and adds not only flavor but a little richness to the dish. Truffle oil can be found in specialty stores and the most esteemed comes from France.

2 tsp.	chopped fresh tarragon	10 mL
1/2 tsp.	chopped fresh basil	2.5 mL
1/2 Tbsp.	lemon, juice and zest	7.5 mL
2 Tbsp.	minced red onion	30 mL
1/4 cup	butter, whipped	60 mL
1/2 tsp.	salt	2.5 mL
1/2 Tbsp.	black pepper	7.5 mL
4	9-oz. (255-g) New York steaks	4
6 Tbsp.	black truffle oil	90 mL
	salt and black pepper to taste	
1 recipe	Brown Sauce	1 recipe

Combine the tarragon, basil, lemon, onion, salt, pepper and butter and mix well. Pipe the butter into rosettes, using a piping bag with a star tip, or roll it into a log and cut off rounds for serving. Wrap in plastic wrap and refrigerate until needed.

Season each steak with 1/2 Tbsp. (7.5 mL) of the truffle oil, salt and pepper. Grill the steaks until they are done to your taste. Top each steak with some herbed butter, 1/4 cup (60 mL) brown sauce and 1 Tbsp. (15 mL) of black truffle oil.

Note: To whip butter, have the butter at room temperature. Place it in a bowl and, using a hand mixer, whip the butter on high speed until it turns almost white. This amount of butter is hard to whip, so fold in the ingredients with a fork (or make a larger quantity and freeze the leftovers).

Brown Sauce

		MAKES 1 CUP (240 ML)
1 1/2 Tbsp.	butter	22.5 mL
1 1/2 Tbsp.	flour	22.5 mL
1 1/2 cups	Brown Stock (see page 59)	360 mL
	salt and black pepper to taste	

In a small saucepan, heat the butter over medium-low heat. When the foam begins to subside, stir in the flour. Turn the heat to low and cook, stirring with a wire whisk almost constantly, until the flour-butter mixture darkens, about 3 minutes. You can cook it longer if you would like a darker color and slightly more complex flavor.

Stir in the stock a little at a time, still using the whisk. When about a cup (240 mL) has been stirred in, the mixture should be fairly thick. Add more stock, a little at a time, until the consistency is just a little thinner than you like, then cook, still over low heat, until it is the consistency you want.

Season to taste and serve immediately or keep warm over gently simmering water for up to an hour, stirring occasionally.

Grilled Sirloin
with Elephant Garlic, Stilton and Red Wine Sauce

I use Black Angus sirloin for this dish. It has been bred to consistently give tender meat. The marbling of the fat, which is created from their diet, tenderizes the meat as it is cooked. I am told 1 in 5 animals make it past the final grading. Sirloin steaks should generally be cooked to no more than medium for best results. If you like your steak well done, just make sure you get your share of sauce. Make sure the wine you drink with this dish is equal to, if not better than, the wine you used for the sauce!

1 Tbsp.	vegetable oil	15 mL
1/4 cup	minced onion	60 mL
1 tsp.	minced garlic	5 mL
1 cup	red wine	240 mL
1 cup	Brown Sauce (see page 89)	240 mL
2 Tbsp.	chopped green onion	30 mL
4	8-oz. (225-g) sirloin steaks, center cut	4
4 Tbsp.	vegetable oil	60 mL
	salt and black pepper to taste	
1	bulb elephant garlic, roasted (see page 13)	1
4	1-oz. (28-g) cubes of Stilton cheese	4

To make the sauce, heat the 1 Tbsp. (15 mL) oil in a sauté pan over medium heat. Add the onion and garlic and cook until the onions are brown. Add the red wine and continue cooking until the volume is reduced to 1/3. Add the brown sauce and green onion. Simmer for 5 minutes and set aside until the steaks are ready.

Brush the steaks with the 4 Tbsp. (60 mL) oil and season with salt and pepper. Heat the grill to high. Grill over high heat for 5 to 7 minutes per side. This will give you a medium-rare to medium steak, depending on the thickness. To finish, top each steak with a large clove of garlic and push the blue cheese down on the garlic. Top with red wine sauce.

Pork Medallions
with Pecans and Maple Bourbon Glaze

Pork can sometimes be dry because many people like it very well done. This sauce keeps the pork moist because the glaze coats the meat.

1 cup	pecan halves	240 mL
2 Tbsp.	maple syrup	30 mL
	pinch salt and black pepper	
2 Tbsp.	butter	30 g
2 Tbsp.	minced onion	30 mL
1 tsp.	minced garlic	5 mL
	salt and black pepper to taste	
1 1/2 cups	maple syrup	360 mL
1/2 recipe	Brown Sauce (see page 89)	1/2 recipe
1/4 cup	bourbon	60 mL
8	3-oz. (85-g) pork tenderloin medallions	8
1/4 cup	oil	60 mL
	salt and black pepper to taste	

Preheat the oven to 350°F (175°C).

Toss the pecans in the 2 Tbsp. (30 mL) maple syrup and season with salt and pepper. Place on a non-stick baking pan and roast for 10 to 15 minutes. Remove from the oven and allow to cool on the pan.

Heat the butter in a sauté pan on medium heat. Add the onion and garlic and cook for 2 minutes. Add the salt, pepper, 1 1/2 cups (360 mL) maple syrup, brown sauce and bourbon. Bring to a simmer and cook until the mixture is reduced by 2/3.

Brush the pork with oil and season with salt and pepper. Grill or pan-fry the medallions over medium-high heat for about 3 minutes on each side. Place the medallions on plates, top with the pecans and spoon the sauce over top.

MEAT AND POULTRY

Oven-Roasted Rack of Lamb
with Pinot Noir Mint Sauce

A whole rack of lamb is a majestic dish. You know that you are splurging when you have one. Mint sauce goes well with lamb because its acidity balances the fat content.

1/2 cup	stone-ground mustard	120 mL
4 Tbsp.	freshly ground peppercorns	60 mL
1 Tbsp.	minced red onion	15 mL
1 Tbsp.	minced garlic	15 mL
1 tsp.	salt	5 mL
1/2 cup	vegetable oil	120 mL
1/4 cup	vegetable oil	60 mL
4	12-oz. (340-g) New Zealand lamb racks	4
1 Tbsp.	minced red onion	15 mL
1 tsp.	minced garlic	5 mL
1/2 cup	Pinot Noir or other red wine	120 mL
1/2 cup	mint sauce	120 mL
1/2 recipe	Brown Sauce (see page 89)	1/2 recipe
	pinch salt and black pepper	
2 Tbsp.	chopped fresh chives	30 mL

To make the marinade, combine the mustard, peppercorns, 1 Tbsp. (15 mL) onion, 1 Tbsp. (15 mL) garlic, salt and 1/2 cup (120 mL) vegetable oil. Pour the marinade over the lamb and marinate in the fridge for at least 1 day (marinate for up to 3 days for a milder lamb flavor).

Preheat the oven to 500°F (260°C).

Heat the 1/4 cup (60 mL) oil in an ovenproof pan over medium-high heat. Sear the racks on both sides. Place in the oven for 7 to 10 minutes. Remove from the pan and let rest while you make the sauce.

Pour out a little of the fat from the pan, leaving about a tablespoon (15 mL). Add the remaining onion and garlic to the pan and cook over medium heat for 1 minute. Add the red wine and mint sauce and simmer for 5 minutes. Add the brown sauce, salt and pepper. Simmer for 2 minutes and add the chives.

Cut the racks into chops or leave them whole. Place on serving plates and pour the sauce over them.

Broiled Double Lamb Chops
with Jalapeño Mint Sauce

I use double-cut chops, which have two bones each, in this recipe. They cook up nice and plump and seem to stay a little moister when cooked. I use chops from the rack here, but chops from the loin or shoulder also work fine.

8	3-oz. (85-g) double rack lamb chops	8
2	cloves garlic, minced	2
	salt and black pepper to taste	
4 Tbsp.	olive oil	60 mL
4 Tbsp.	butter	60 mL
1/2 cup	minced onion	120 mL
1/2 cup	minced jalapeño	120 mL
1/2 cup	chopped fresh mint	120 mL
1/4 cup	sweet red vermouth	60 mL
1/4 cup	chopped fresh parsley	60 mL
1/4 cup	chopped fresh chives	60 mL
1/2 tsp.	salt	2.5 mL
1/2 tsp.	black pepper	2.5 mL
1/4 lb.	cold butter, cut into 1/2-inch (1.2-cm) cubes	113 g

Rub the lamb chops with the garlic, salt, pepper and oil. Refrigerate overnight.

Melt the 4 Tbsp. (60 mL) butter over medium heat and sauté the onion, jalapeño and mint for 2 minutes. Deglaze with the vermouth. Add the parsley, chives, salt and pepper. Whisk in the butter all at once and remove from the heat when it's melted.

Preheat the broiler. Place the chops in a broiling pan and place in the middle of the oven. Broil the lamb chops for 5 to 7 minutes on each side. Place on plates, pour the sauce over top and serve immediately.

MEAT AND POULTRY

93

Chicken Breast
with Pancetta and Aniseed Sauce

Chicken ranks as one of the world's most popular dishes. The pancetta in this dish adds flavor and richness. We like to leave the wing tip on the breast for the presentation. Ask your local butcher for this cut.

1/4 cup	olive oil	60 mL
4	9-oz. (255-g) boneless chicken breasts, wing tip on	4
	salt and black pepper to taste	
8	thin slices pancetta, about 1 oz. (28 g) each	8
1/4 cup	minced onion	60 mL
1 tsp.	minced garlic	5 mL
1 Tbsp.	aniseed	15 mL
1/4 cup	white wine	60 mL
1/2 recipe	Brown Sauce (see page 89)	1/2 recipe
	salt and black pepper to taste	
2 Tbsp.	chopped fresh chives	30 mL

Preheat the oven to 450°F (230°C).

Heat the olive oil in an ovenproof frying pan over medium-high heat. Season the chicken breasts with salt and pepper and brown them in the oil, skin side down. Move them around in the pan to get an even, crisp, dark brown skin. Add the pancetta, onion, garlic and aniseed. Sauté for a couple of minutes. Turn the chicken over and add the white wine. Stir, scraping up the bits from the bottom of pan. Pour half of the brown sauce over the chicken.

Place the pan in the oven and bake for 10 minutes. Check the chicken once in a while to make sure there is liquid in the pan. After 10 minutes there should only be about 10% of the liquid left. Remove the pan and add a splash more wine or brown sauce if the sauce is too dry.

Remove the chicken and keep it warm while you finish the sauce. Add the rest of the brown sauce, salt, pepper and chives to the pan. Bring back to a simmer. Stir well and spoon over the chicken.

MEAT AND POULTRY

Almond-Crusted Chicken
with Tandoori Fried Onions and Mango Mustard Purée

The almonds give the chicken a nutty flavor, the tandoori onion spices it up and the mango mustard purée rounds out the dish with a little coolness.

2 cups	sliced onion	475 mL
1/2 cup	tandoori paste	120 mL
1/4 cup	flour	60 mL
1/2 tsp.	salt	2.5 mL
1/2 tsp.	black pepper	2.5 mL
1/2 tsp.	ground cumin	2.5 mL
1/2 tsp.	ground coriander	2.5 mL
4	6-oz. (170-g) boneless, skinless chicken legs, including thighs	4
2	large eggs, beaten	2
1 cup	medium-ground almonds	240 mL
1/4 cup	vegetable oil	60 mL
1 cup	mango purée	240 mL
1 Tbsp.	Dijon mustard	15 mL
1 Tbsp.	grainy mustard	15 mL
4	sprigs fresh cilantro	4

Marinate the onion in the tandoori paste for at least 1 hour. Preheat the oven to 325°F (165°C).

Combine the flour, salt, pepper, cumin and coriander. Coat the chicken with the mixture. Brush one side of each chicken piece with egg and coat with the ground almonds.

Heat the oil in an ovenproof pan over medium heat. Add the chicken legs, almond side down, and fry to a golden brown. Turn the legs. Place the pan in the oven and bake for about 10 minutes. Remove from the oven and check for doneness. You should not see any pink but it should be juicy. Remove the chicken from the pan and keep warm.

Add the marinated onion to the pan and sauté over medium-high heat until browned, about 5 minutes. Divide the onions evenly over the chicken. Combine the mango purée and mustards and spoon it over the chicken and onions. Garnish with fresh cilantro.

MEAT AND POULTRY

Prawn-Stuffed Chicken Breast
with Lemon Tarragon Butter Sauce

Chicken and prawns complement each other. They are both mild in taste and neither overpowers the other.

4	9-oz. (225-g) boneless chicken breasts, skin on	4
1 recipe	Hollandaise Sauce	1 recipe
4	tiger prawns, 16/20 count (see page 119), shelled and deveined (see page 121)	4
3 Tbsp.	chopped fresh tarragon	45 mL
1/4 cup	olive oil	60 mL
1/4 cup	minced onion	60 mL
1 tsp.	minced garlic	5 mL
1 cup	white wine	240 mL
2 Tbsp.	lemon juice	30 mL
1/2 lb.	cold butter, cut into 1-inch (2.5-cm) cubes	225 g
1/2 tsp.	salt	2.5 mL
1 tsp.	black pepper	5 mL

In each chicken breast, make a cut that's big enough for the prawn to fit into. Put 1 Tbsp. (15 mL) of hollandaise in each opening. Wash the prawns and pat them dry. Season with a little salt, pepper and 1 Tbsp. (15 mL) of the tarragon. Push a prawn into each opening.

Preheat the oven to 450°F (230°C). Heat the olive oil in a roasting pan that's just large enough to hold the four breasts. Season the breasts with salt and pepper and place them skin side down in the pan. Brown over medium-high heat. Turn the chicken over and add the onion and garlic. Sauté for 1 minute, then add 1/2 cup (120 mL) of the wine. Place in the oven and bake for 10 to 12 minutes.

Remove the pan and transfer the chicken to a plate. Keep warm.

To finish the sauce, add the remaining white wine and the lemon juice to the pan. Cook over high heat until the liquid is reduced to about 1/4 cup (60 mL). Add the remaining tarragon and hollandaise and whisk in the butter. Season with salt and pepper. Ladle the sauce over the breasts and serve immediately.

Hollandaise Sauce

MAKES ABOUT ¹/₂ CUP (120 ML)

2	egg yolks	2
1 Tbsp.	vinegar	15 mL
1 Tbsp.	water	15 mL
1 Tbsp.	minced onion	15 mL
1	small bay leaf	1
¹/₃ cup	clarified butter (see page 44)	80 mL
1 tsp.	lemon juice	5 mL
	pinch cayenne pepper	
	salt and black pepper to taste	

Mix the egg yolks, vinegar, water, onion and bay leaf in a stainless steel bowl. Place over a simmering pot of water. I usually like the bowl to sit in the water because if it sits above the simmering water you are using the steam to cook the eggs, which I feel is too hot. Cook and whisk the mixture for about 3 to 5 minutes, until it almost doubles in volume. Remove from the heat and slowly whisk in the butter a little at a time, adding it especially slowly at the beginning. Mix in the lemon juice, cayenne, salt and pepper. Remove the bay leaf before serving.

Chicken Stuffed
with Wild Mushroom Ragôut

The wild mushrooms go well with the stronger flavor of the leg meat. These can be made up to a day ahead. The bundles also freeze well.

4	7-oz. (200-g) boneless chicken legs with thigh	4
	salt and black pepper to taste	
2 cups	sliced mixed shiitake, portobello and oyster mushrooms	475 mL
1/2 cup	olive oil	120 mL
1/2 cup	minced onion	120 mL
1 Tbsp.	minced garlic	15 mL
2 Tbsp.	tomato paste	30 mL
1/2 cup	diced zucchini or eggplant	120 mL
1 cup	white wine	240 mL
1/4 cup	tomato concasse (see page 99)	60 mL
2 Tbsp.	chopped fresh basil	30 mL
2 Tbsp.	chopped fresh chives	30 mL
1 Tbsp.	chopped fresh thyme	15 mL
1 Tbsp.	chopped fresh oregano	15 mL

Place the chicken between 2 layers of plastic wrap and pound it until it's about 1/3 inch (.8 cm) thick. Place it skin side down and season with salt and pepper.

Place the olive oil in a pan over high heat. Add the mushrooms and stir and toss for about 10 minutes. You want to sear the mushrooms, rather than boiling them in their juices. Add the onion, garlic, tomato paste and zucchini or eggplant. Reduce the heat to medium-high and sauté for 1 to 2 minutes. Add the white wine and continue cooking to reduce the liquid to about 1/4 cup (60 mL). Stir in the tomato concasse and herbs. If the mixture is too runny (that is, if you see more than about a tablespoon (15 mL) of liquid), reduce it until it's thick over medium heat. Cool to room temperature.

Preheat the oven to 400°F (200°C). Divide the mushroom ragôut into 4 portions. Place one portion in the center of each piece of chicken, skin side on the outside. Wrap the chicken around the ragôut and place on a roasting pan, open end down. To hold the chicken together while cooking, oil a piece of aluminum foil and wrap it around each chicken portion.

Place the roasting pan in the center of the oven. Lower the heat to 350°F (175°C) and cook for 7 minutes. Remove the foil and continue cooking for another 8 minutes. You can serve the chicken whole or slice each serving into 2 or 3 medallions.

TOMATO CONCASSE

Concasse is widely used in every restaurant kitchen. In the French language concasse means "roughly chopped." Tomato concasse is made of diced tomatoes that have had the stems, seeds and skin removed.

Pan-Seared Duck Breast
with Blueberry Cognac Sauce

This is a great combination with either duck or pork. Use your favorite brandy—they all have their own flavors and strengths. I was weaned on the apple-flavored Calvados but Armagnac is also nice, and using your best cognac is not a waste.

4	10-oz. (285-g) duck breasts with rib and breast bone	4
4 Tbsp.	seasoning salt	60 mL
1/4 cup	rendered duck fat or olive oil	60 mL
1/4 cup	minced onion	60 mL
1 cup	sweet white wine	240 mL
1 cup	blueberries	240 mL
1/2 cup	Brown Sauce (see page 89)	120 mL
1/4 cup	brandy	60 mL
1/4 cup	chopped fresh chives	60 mL

Heavily season the duck skin. Preheat the oven to 450°F (230°C).

Heat the duck fat or olive oil over medium heat in a roasting pan just large enough to hold the 4 breasts. Place the breasts skin side down in the pan and cook until the skin is totally brown. Turn the breasts over, add the onion and 1/2 cup (120 mL) of the wine. Place in the oven and bake for 8 minutes. Remove the duck from the pan and keep it warm while you finish the sauce. Drain the excess oil from the roasting pan leaving about 1 tsp. (5 mL).

Purée 1/4 of the blueberries with the remaining 1/2 cup (120 mL) of wine. Add this to the pan, along with the brown sauce and brandy. Cook until it's reduced by 1/3 and add the chives.

Remove the duck meat from the bone and remove the skin. Slice 1 or 2 of the duck skins into thin strips and fry until crisp in a little oil over medium heat. Slice the breasts into thin medallions and divide them among 4 plates. Cover with the sauce and scatter the fried duck skin (crackling) over top.

MEAT AND POULTRY

Fish and Seafood

Plank-Baked Salmon
with Pear and Rosemary Vinaigrette

You might have heard of cooking on cedar planks, but here at the Salmon House we prefer alder. The smell of the hot alder is wonderful. Fresh-cut green wood is best because it smokes better and takes longer to burn.

4	8-oz. (225-g) boneless salmon fillets, skin on	4
4 Tbsp.	melted butter	60 mL
$1/2$–1 cup	Pear and Rosemary Vinaigrette	120–240 mL

Soak 2 alder planks, 8 inches (20 cm) across and 1 inch (2.5 cm) thick, in water for at least 1 hour. Preheat the oven to 400°F (200°C).

Place 2 salmon fillets on each plank, brush them with butter and bake for 10 minutes. To serve, place on individual plates and spoon the vinaigrette over the salmon.

Pear and Rosemary Vinaigrette

		MAKES 1 $1/2$ CUPS (360 ML)
1	Bartlett pear, cored, stemmed and medium diced	1
$1/4$ cup	diced red onion	60 mL
$1/4$ cup	malt vinegar	60 mL
$1/2$ Tbsp.	honey	7.5 mL
	pinch salt	
$1/2$ tsp.	black pepper	2.5 mL
$1/4$ cup	rosemary oil	60 mL
$1/4$ cup	olive oil	60 mL

Mix the pear, onion, vinegar, honey, salt and pepper in a mixing bowl. Combine the oils and slowly whisk into the mixture. Serve at room temperature.

This vinaigrette can be refrigerated for up to a week. Leftovers can be served on salads or other fish.

FISH AND SEAFOOD

Grilled Chili-Crusted Salmon
with Tomato Balsamic Salsa and Tortilla Chips

This dish is light enough to be served for lunch or dinner. Tortilla chips are very easy to make, but your favorite store-bought variety will also work well. Placing the salsa on top of the salmon will cool it down, so make sure the salmon is served as hot as possible.

2 Tbsp.	white pepper	30 mL
3 Tbsp.	ground cinnamon	45 mL
3 Tbsp.	ground ginger	45 mL
1/2 cup	Demerara sugar	120 mL
1/4 cup	red wine vinegar	60 mL
2 Tbsp.	sesame oil	30 mL
1/2 cup	peanut oil	120 mL
3 Tbsp.	fennel seeds	45 mL
3 Tbsp.	puréed chipotle peppers	45 mL
2 Tbsp.	chili powder	30 mL
4	8-oz. (225-g) boneless salmon fillets, skin on	4
16	Tortilla Chips (see page 105)	16
1/2 recipe	Tomato Balsamic Salsa (see page 104)	1/2 recipe

To make the marinade, place the pepper, cinnamon, ginger, sugar, vinegar, oils, fennel, chipotle peppers and chili powder in a medium saucepan. Bring to a boil, remove from the heat and cool before using.

Brush the salmon generously with the marinade and refrigerate for 4 to 6 hours or overnight.

Preheat the oven to 400°F (200°C). Bake the salmon for 6 minutes. (Or barbecue for 4 to 5 minutes per side over high heat.) Cut each piece into 4 and keep warm.

To serve, place 4 tortilla chips on each plate, place a piece of salmon on each and some salsa on top.

FISH AND SEAFOOD

103

Tomato Balsamic Salsa

		MAKES 2 CUPS (475 ML)
1 cup	tomato concasse (see page 99)	475 mL
1/2 cup	diced red onion	240 mL
1/2 cup	balsamic vinegar	240 mL
1 tsp.	lemon, juice only	5 mL
	pinch salt	
1/2 tsp.	black pepper	2.5 mL
1 Tbsp.	chopped fresh basil	15 mL
2 tsp.	chopped fresh parsley	10 mL
1 Tbsp.	chopped chives or scallion	15 mL
2 Tbsp.	olive oil	30 mL

Place everything in a mixing bowl except for the oil. Toss well and fold in the oil. Let it sit for at least 2 hours before using.

Leftover salsa can be used as a vegetable dip or mixed in with salads. It can be stored in the refrigerator for up to 1 week.

Tortilla Chips

1 1/2 cups	corn flour	360 mL
	pinch salt	
3/4 cup	warm water	180 mL

Place the corn flour and salt in a bowl. Add the water slowly, kneading until a smooth dough is formed. Divide into 14 pieces and let stand for 1 hour.

Place a piece of dough between two sheets of plastic wrap. Flatten with a rolling pin into a thin cake, 5 inches (12.5 cm) in diameter. Heat an ungreased, heavy pan until hot and place a tortilla in the pan. Cook for about 1 minute or until golden specks appear on the tortilla's surface. Turn the tortilla over and cook on the other side for 1 to 1 1/2 minutes. Wrap in a warm cloth and keep hot while cooking the other tortillas.

Heat 2 inches (5 cm) of oil in a wide, 8 to 9 1/2-quart (8 to 9.5 L) pot over moderately high heat until a deep-fat thermometer registers 375°F (190°C). Cut each tortilla into quarters. When the oil is hot, fry the tortilla pieces, keeping a good space between the chips. Turn the chips and fry until crisp on the other side. Remove from the pan, drain on paper towels and keep hot. Store the extra tortilla chips in an airtight container. They should keep for 2 weeks. Reheating them in an oven at 350°F (175°C) for 2 minutes will bring them back to their original state of freshness.

Juniper Berry Spiked Salmon Steaks
with Raspberry Coulis

This is a very bright-looking dish with the dark orange sockeye salmon and the rich red raspberry coulis. Juniper berries come from a bush that grows wild in woods and mountain gullies. The berries are used to season marinades, especially for game. They are available dried at many grocery stores and specialty stores. They are also used in the distillation of gin.

4	8-oz. (225-g) sockeye salmon steaks	4
32	dried juniper berries	32
4 Tbsp.	olive oil	60 mL
	salt and black pepper to taste	
2 cups	raspberries	475 mL
1 cup	simple syrup (see page 169)	240 mL
1 Tbsp.	lemon juice	15 mL
1/2 tsp.	salt	2.5 mL
1/2 tsp.	black pepper	2.5 mL
1/2 tsp.	paprika	2.5 mL
4 Tbsp.	chopped fresh chives	60 mL

Press 4 juniper berries into each side of the salmon steaks. Make sure they break the surface and don't just sit on top because they will fall off. Brush with oil and grill over medium-high heat for 10 minutes per inch (2.5 cm). Season with salt and pepper.

To make the coulis, place the raspberries, syrup, lemon juice, salt, pepper and paprika in a blender and liquefy. Strain out the seeds.

Spoon the coulis over the salmon, add a few chopped chives and serve immediately.

Rum-Soaked Salmon
with Apple Ginger Purée

We have been soaking salmon in rum for a long time at the Salmon House. Salmon is rich from its own oils and absorb marinades very well. The rum and sugar almost candy the salmon as it marinates.

1/4 cup	dark rum	60 mL
2 Tbsp.	Demerara sugar	30 mL
1 Tbsp.	minced lemon grass (white part only)	15 mL
	salt and black pepper to taste	
4	8-oz. (225-g) boneless salmon fillets	4
1 recipe	Apple Ginger Purée	1 recipe

Mix together the rum, sugar, lemon grass, salt and pepper and rub the mixture over the salmon. Marinate for at least 4 hours or overnight. Turn the salmon over frequently for best results.

Preheat the oven to 400°F (200°C). Bake the salmon for 10 minutes. Remove the salmon, place on serving plates and top with Apple Ginger Purée. The purée is served cold, so if you don't want anyone to complain about cold salmon, serve it on the side or around the salmon rather than on top.

Apple Ginger Purée

MAKES 1 1/2 CUPS (360 ML)

1 Tbsp.	granulated sugar	15 mL
2 Tbsp.	hot water	30 mL
1/2 cup	ginger, peeled and finely grated	120 mL
1 cup	peeled and diced Granny Smith apple	240 mL
1 Tbsp.	apricot chutney	15 mL
1 Tbsp.	white wine	15 mL
1/2 tsp.	Dijon mustard	2.5 mL

Dissolve the sugar in the hot water. Combine the ginger, apple, chutney, white wine, mustard and sugar solution. Process in a food processor until finely ground. Store in the refrigerator until needed.

FISH AND SEAFOOD

Chilean Sea Bass
with Pistachio Prawn Butter and Crisp Potato Galettes

Chilean sea bass is an oily fish that has nice big flakes. At the Salmon House we almost always grill it, but we've been known to steam or poach it every now and then. I like to grill it because the oils drip into the fire and it almost bastes itself.

1/4 cup	oil	60 mL
4	7-oz. (200-g) sea bass fillets	4
1 recipe	Crisp Potato Galettes	1 recipe
1 recipe	Pistachio Prawn Butter	1 recipe
	pinch salt and black pepper	
2 Tbsp.	chopped chives	30 mL

Heat the oil over medium-high heat, add the fish and cook for 5 to 10 minutes, turning it halfway through the cooking. Place a galette on each plate and put a fillet in the center. Top with the prawn butter and sprinkle with chives.

Pistachio Prawn Butter

		MAKES 1 CUP (240 ML)
4	tiger prawns, 26/30 count (see page 119)	4
1 Tbsp.	olive oil	15 mL
2 Tbsp.	minced red onion	30 mL
1 tsp.	minced garlic	5 mL
1 tsp.	lemon zest	5 mL
3 Tbsp.	pistachio nuts, blanched	45 mL
1/2 tsp.	lemon pepper	2.5 mL
1/5 tsp.	salt	1 mL
1 tsp.	lemon juice	5 mL
1/2 cup	salted butter, at room temperature	120 mL
1 tsp.	chopped fresh dill	5 mL
2 Tbsp.	thinly sliced green onions	30 mL

Peel, devein and roughly chop the prawns. Heat the olive oil over medium heat, add the prawns and sauté for 2 minutes, until red and plump. (Do not overcook.) Add the onion, garlic, lemon zest, pistachios, lemon pepper and salt. Simmer for 2 minutes and add the lemon juice. Remove from the heat and cool.

When the prawn mixture is cool, combine it with the softened butter. Fold in the dill and green onions, mixing well. Place the butter on waxed paper and roll the paper around it to form a cylinder shape, or log. Refrigerate for 1 hour. When the butter has hardened, it can be cut into medallions, or rounds.

Crisp Potato Galettes

		MAKES 4
2 cups	grated potato, peeled or unpeeled	475 mL
2 Tbsp.	minced onion	30 mL
1/2 tsp.	salt	2.5 mL
1 tsp.	black pepper	5 mL
1/4 cup	oil	60 mL

Rinse the grated potato in water until the starch is gone and the water runs clear. Squeeze out the water. Toss the potato with the onion, salt and pepper. Heat 1 Tbsp. (15 mL) of the oil in a frying pan over high heat. (Non-stick is best because the galette will stick if the heat is not high enough.) Place 1/4 of the potato mixture in the pan and fry until the edges are dark brown, then carefully flip it over. Turn it away from yourself, so if oil splashes, it is not towards you. Fry the other side until it is brown and crusty. Remove and drain on paper towel. Repeat with the remaining mixture.

Striped Bass
with Red Grapes, Lemon and Maple Butter Sauce

This is a great fish for frying, and if you remove the scales you can eat it like trout, skin and all. The sauce is mildly sweet and goes well with the fried fish.

2 Tbsp.	flour	30 mL
1 tsp.	salt	5 mL
2 tsp.	black pepper	10 mL
4	7-oz. (200-g) striped bass fillets	4
6 Tbsp.	butter	90 mL
1 Tbsp.	butter	15 mL
2 Tbsp.	minced onion	30 mL
2 Tbsp.	maple syrup	30 mL
2 Tbsp.	lemon juice	30 mL
1 cup	white wine	240 mL
1 cup	red seedless grapes, cut in half	240 mL
3 Tbsp.	whipping cream	45 mL
1/2 lb.	cold unsalted butter, cubed	225 g
2 Tbsp.	chopped fresh chives	30 mL
	salt and black pepper to taste	

Preheat the oven to 400°F (200°C).

Mix the flour, salt and pepper together. Coat the fish with the mixture. Heat the 6 Tbsp. (90 mL) butter in an ovenproof pan over medium heat and fry the bass skin side up in the butter. Turn the fish over, place the pan in the oven and bake for 5 minutes. Remove the fish from the pan and keep warm.

Add the 1 Tbsp. (15 mL) butter, minced onion and maple syrup to the pan and cook for 2 minutes over medium heat. Add the lemon juice, wine and grapes. Continue to cook until the sauce is reduced to 1/4 cup (60 mL). Add the whipping cream and bring to a boil. Remove from the heat and whisk in the cubed butter and chives.

Place the bass on individual plates and spoon the butter sauce over the fish.

Pan-Roasted Halibut
with Almond Dill Pesto

Halibut is a beautiful fish. The meat is rich, white and flakes into large pieces. Halibut goes well with cream sauces.

1 cup	whipping cream	240 mL
4 Tbsp.	Almond Dill Pesto	60 mL
4 Tbsp.	grated Parmesan cheese	60 mL
4	8-oz. (225-g) halibut fillets	4
4 Tbsp.	olive oil	60 mL
	salt and black pepper to taste	

Place the cream and pesto in a saucepan over medium heat and stir until it's well mixed. When it comes to a boil add the cheese. Reduce to a simmer.

Preheat the oven to 400°F (200°C). Brush the halibut with the olive oil and season with salt and pepper. Bake for 8 minutes. Serve with generous amounts of the sauce on top.

Almond Dill Pesto

MAKES 1 TO 1 1/2 CUPS (240 TO 360 ML)		
1 cup	chopped fresh dill	240 mL
1/2 cup	slivered almonds, toasted	120 mL
1/4 cup	chopped fresh parsley	60 mL
1 tsp.	salt	5 mL
1 Tbsp.	black pepper	15 mL
1 tsp.	minced garlic	5 mL
1/3 cup	olive oil	80 mL

Combine the dill, almonds, parsley, salt, pepper and garlic in a food processor. Process until finely chopped. Slowly add the oil.

Pesto will keep for 2 weeks in the refrigerator, or you can freeze it in ice-cube trays. Leftovers can be used to garnish pizzas, soup or vegetables.

FISH AND SEAFOOD

111

Mustard Seed Crusted Ahi Tuna
with Caper Brown Butter Sauce

A dusting of mustard seed allows the delicious taste of the tuna to shine in this easy to make dish.

4	7-oz. (200-g) ahi tuna fillets	4
4 Tbsp.	olive oil	60 mL
1/2 cup	mustard seeds	120 mL
	pinch salt and black pepper	
4 Tbsp.	minced onion	60 mL
1/2 cup	capers	120 mL
2 Tbsp.	lemon juice	30 mL
1/2 cup	butter	120 mL

Brush both sides of the tuna with a little of the oil, and cover with the mustard seeds. Season with salt and pepper. Heat the remaining oil in a sauté pan over medium-high heat. Add the tuna and cook for 2 minutes on each side. Remove to a warm plate.

Add the onion and capers to the pan and sauté until the onion is lightly browned. Add the lemon juice. Turn the heat to high and add the butter. Cook for 1 to 2 minutes, until the butter bubbles up and turns brown. Pour the sauce over the tuna and serve immediately.

Cheese-Crusted Sole
with Papaya Pink Peppercorn Cream

Sole is a mild-tasting, delicate fish that pairs well with the flavorful cheese crust in this dish.

4	6-oz. (170-g) sole fillets	4
1/2 tsp.	salt	2.5 mL
1/2 tsp.	black pepper	2.5 mL
3 Tbsp.	oil	45 mL
1/4 cup	grated Parmesan cheese	60 mL
1/4 cup	grated Asiago cheese	60 mL
16	pink peppercorns, cracked	16
1/2 tsp.	salt	2.5 mL
1/4 cup	diced papaya	60 mL
1/4 cup	Cointreau or other orange liqueur	60 mL
2 cups	whipping cream	475 mL

Preheat the oven to 400°F (200°C).

Season the sole with salt and pepper and roll each fillet up. (Rolling it up protects the delicate texture and makes a nice presentation.) Heat the oil in an ovenproof sauté pan over medium heat and sear the sole. Combine the cheeses. Top the sole with the cheese mixture, place in the oven and bake for 8 minutes.

Remove the sole from the pan to a warm plate. Drain the excess oil from the pan and add the peppercorns, salt, papaya, Cointreau and cream. Cook over medium-high heat until the sauce is reduced by half. Spoon the sauce over the sole.

FISH AND SEAFOOD

Alaska Black Cod
with Curry, Apple and Carrot Butter and Ginger Couscous

Black cod is rich in oils and has a wonderful smoked flavor. The curry sauce is very colorful and adds a little spice to the dish.

2 cups	water	475 mL
1/4 cup	ginger wine	60 mL
1/2 tsp.	minced fresh ginger	2.5 mL
2 Tbsp.	chopped green onion	30 mL
4	8-oz. (225-g) smoked black cod fillets	4
1 recipe	Ginger Couscous	1 recipe
1 recipe	Curry, Apple and Carrot Butter	1 recipe

Combine the water, ginger wine and ginger in a small pot and bring to a simmer. Add the green onion. Place the cod on a steaming rack over the stock and cover. Cook for 7 to 10 minutes.

To serve, press the couscous into a 4-inch (10-cm) ring mold, then unmold in the center of the plate. Top with the steamed cod. Pour the butter sauce around the couscous.

Curry, Apple and Carrot Butter

		MAKES 1 CUP (240 ML)
4 Tbsp.	unsalted butter	60 mL
4 Tbsp.	minced onion	60 mL
4 Tbsp.	minced apple	60 mL
4 tsp.	curry powder	20 mL
1/2 cup	unsalted butter	120 mL
1/2 cup	carrot juice	120 mL
	salt and black pepper to taste	

Melt the 4 Tbsp. (60 mL) butter over low heat and stew the onion, apple and curry powder for 10 minutes or so. Cool and blend in a food processor for about 30 seconds. Add the remaining 1/2 cup (120 mL) of butter and process for another 30 seconds or so. Place on plastic wrap, form into a block and refrigerate. (I refrigerate the butter because cold butter emulsifies into a hot liquid better than warm butter.)

Dice the butter. Bring the carrot juice to a boil and whisk in the flavored butter. Season with salt and pepper. Take the sauce off the heat as soon as the butter is melted.

Ginger Couscous

		SERVES 4
2 Tbsp.	olive oil	30 mL
1 cup	minced onion	240 mL
2 Tbsp.	minced ginger	30 mL
1 1/2 cups	couscous	360 mL
1/2 tsp.	salt	2.5 mL
1/4 tsp.	black pepper	1.2 mL
1 1/2 cups	water	360 mL

Heat the oil over medium heat, add the onion and ginger and sauté for 1 minute. Stir in the couscous, salt and pepper. Add the water and bring to a boil. Stir and simmer for 1 minute. Turn down to very low, cover and let sit for 5 minutes.

Garlic-Crusted Ling Cod
with Prawns in Red Pepper Sauce

Here is a dish based on an inexpensive local fish. The prawns in red pepper sauce make an excellent garnish.

2 cups	diced fresh baguette	475 mL
1 tsp.	salt	5 mL
1 tsp.	black pepper	5 mL
2 Tbsp.	grated Parmesan cheese	30 mL
1 tsp.	minced garlic	5 mL
1 tsp.	minced fresh thyme	5 mL
4	5-oz. (140-g) boneless, skinless cod fillets	4
6 Tbsp.	oil	90 mL
4 Tbsp.	butter	60 mL
1 recipe	Prawns in Red Pepper Sauce	1 recipe

Preheat the oven to 400°F (200°C).

Pulse the diced bread in a food processor until fine crumbs are formed. Add the salt, pepper, cheese, garlic and thyme and process for 10 seconds. Coat the cod with the mixture, pressing it on firmly.

Heat the oil in an ovenproof pan over medium heat. Place the cod crumb side down in the pan. After about 1 minute add the butter and let it brown. Turn the fish over, place it in the oven and bake for 7 minutes. The fish should still be moist and the breading should be brown and crisp.

To serve, cover half the cod with sauce and prawns. This presentation allows the bread crumbs on the other half to stay crisp.

Prawns in Red Pepper Sauce

		SERVES 4
1/4 cup	olive oil	60 mL
3/4 cup	roasted red pepper (see page 183)	180 mL
1/4 cup	tomato concasse (see page 99)	60 mL
1/2 cup	minced onion	120 mL
	pinch cayenne pepper	
4 tsp.	lemon juice	20 mL
4 tsp.	lime juice	20 mL
12	tiger prawns, shelled and deveined (see page 121)	12
1 cup	Salmon Stock (see page 56)	240 mL

Heat the olive oil in a saucepan over medium heat. Add the red pepper, tomato, onion and cayenne pepper. Simmer for 1 minute and add the lemon juice, lime juice and prawns. Add the stock and simmer for 5 minutes, or until the sauce is thick.

Vancouver Island Sidestripe Prawns
with Chili Almond Pesto

Six shrimp species thrive off the coast of British Columbia. This type gets its name from the stripes on the shells. They are not farmed like other prawns and the catch is small. When fresh, they are very sweet and tender. If the heads are black, don't use them—it means they are old.

1/4 cup	olive oil	60 mL
2.2 lbs.	fresh prawns, shelled and deveined (see page 121), washed under cold water for 10 minutes to thoroughly clean them	1 kg
1/2 cup	minced onion	120 mL
1 recipe	Chili Almond Pesto	1 recipe
1/2 cup	vegetable stock (see page 58)	120 mL
1/2 cup	whipping cream	120 mL
1/4 cup	chopped green onion	60 mL

In a heavy frying pan, heat the oil over high heat. Add the prawns, cooking and tossing for 2 minutes. Add the onion and pesto, breaking up the pesto with a fork. Add the vegetable stock and simmer for 2 minutes. Add the cream and cook for 3 to 5 minutes. Add the green onion and serve immediately.

Chili Almond Pesto

		MAKES 1 1/2 CUPS (360 ML)
1 Tbsp.	sambal oelek	15 mL
1 tsp.	lime juice	5 mL
1 tsp.	lemon juice	5 mL
1/2 tsp.	minced fresh ginger	2.5 mL
1/2 tsp.	ground coriander	2.5 mL
1/4 tsp.	ground cumin	1.2 mL
1 tsp.	minced garlic	5 mL
1/4 cup	diced onion	60 mL
1/2 tsp.	salt	2.5 mL
1 tsp.	black pepper	5 mL
1 cup	blanched almonds	240 mL
1/4 cup	olive oil	60 mL

Place the sambal oelek, lime juice, lemon juice, ginger, coriander, cumin, garlic, onion, salt, pepper and almonds in the food processor. Pulse until it's coarsely chopped. Slowly add the oil with the machine running until you have a smooth paste.

BUYING PRAWNS AND SCALLOPS

Prawns and scallops can be bought not only large or small but also by the number per pound (455 grams). An example would be 10 count— that means there are 10 prawns of approximately the same weight in a pound (455 grams). A 26/30 count means that there are 26 to 30 with equal weight in a pound (455 grams). Buying them this way allows you to buy items that are more consistent in size, which helps in cooking and portioning.

Shrimp and Lobster
with Spinach, Couscous and Dill Sauce

I love any kind of lobster, and shrimp only makes it better. This is a deliciously fast dish to make. Serve it with a sprig of dill and a wedge of lemon.

FOR THE COUSCOUS:

1/2 cup	minced onion	120 mL
1 1/2 cups	couscous	360 mL
1/2 tsp.	salt	2.5 mL
1/4 tsp.	black pepper	1.2 mL
2 Tbsp.	olive oil	30 mL
1 1/2 cups	water	360 mL

Sauté the onion, couscous, salt and pepper in the olive oil over medium heat for 1 minute. Add the water and bring to a boil. Stir and simmer for 1 minute. Turn the heat to very low, cover and let sit for 5 minutes. Divide the couscous among 4 plates.

FOR THE DILL SAUCE:

2 Tbsp.	olive oil	30 mL
2 Tbsp.	minced onion	30 mL
1/2 cup	chopped fresh dill	120 mL
1/2 tsp.	salt	2.5 mL
1/2 tsp.	black pepper	2.5 mL
2 cups	heavy cream	475 mL

Heat the oil over medium heat and sauté the onion, dill, salt and pepper for 1 minute. Add the cream and cook until it's reduced by half.

TO ASSEMBLE THE DISH:

4 Tbsp.	olive oil	60 mL
2	8-oz. (225-g) lobster tails, shell removed	2
4 Tbsp.	minced onion	60 mL
1 tsp.	minced garlic	5 mL
2 Tbsp.	lemon juice	30 mL
1/2 tsp.	salt	2.5 mL
1 tsp.	black pepper	5 mL
1 lb.	spinach, blanched	455 g
12 oz.	baby shrimp	340 g
1/2 cup	white wine	120 mL
2 Tbsp.	butter	30 mL

Heat the oil in a large saucepan over medium heat. Add the lobster, onion and garlic and sauté for 1 minute. Add the lemon juice, salt, pepper and spinach. Mix well and add the shrimp and white wine. Bring to a simmer and cook until the liquid is reduced by half. Add the butter, toss and mix well. Place the seafood over the couscous. Pour the dill sauce over the seafood.

PEELING AND DEVEINING SHRIMP

Shrimp should be peeled if it will be cooked in a sauce that will make it difficult to peel them at the table. For simple grilling or pan-cooking, however, it's arguable that shrimp with their shells lose less liquid and flavor. Some people won't eat shrimp that isn't deveined. Others believe that the vein —actually the animal's intestinal tract— contributes to flavor. It's a matter of personal taste; devein only if you choose to.

Scallop Ravioli
with Three-Cheese Alfredo and Basil Pesto

The ravioli sheets in this dish have the texture of the top of a lasagna, crisp and cheesy.

8	4 x 4-inch (10 x 10-cm) egg pasta squares	8
1/4 cup	vegetable oil	60 mL
	salt and black pepper to taste	
1/4 cup	olive oil	60 mL
32	scallops, 20/30 count (see page 119)	32
4 Tbsp.	minced onion	60 mL
1 Tbsp.	minced garlic	15 mL
1/2 tsp.	salt	2.5 mL
1/2 tsp.	black pepper	2.5 mL
1/4 cup	white wine	60 mL
1 1/2 cups	whipping cream	360 mL
2 Tbsp.	grated Parmesan cheese	30 mL
2 Tbsp.	grated Asiago cheese	30 mL
2 Tbsp.	grated white Cheddar cheese	30 mL
4 tsp.	chopped fresh chives	20 mL
1/4 cup	Basil Pesto	60 mL

Blanch the pasta in salted water for 4 minutes. Remove, drain, and toss in the vegetable oil. Season with salt and pepper. Heat the oil in a sauté pan over medium-high heat. Add the pasta and fry for about 3 to 5 minutes per side. Watch for the bubbles to appear; this tells you it's time to turn the sheets. Do not allow them to get too crisp.

Heat the olive oil in a pan over medium-high heat. Pat the scallops dry, add them to the pan and sear for 5 minutes. Add the onion, garlic, salt and pepper. Cook until the onions and garlic are slightly brown. Add the white wine and deglaze the pan. Remove the scallops and add 1 cup (240 mL) of the cream. Bring to a boil and add half the cheese. Cook until the mixture is reduced by half. Return the scallops to the pan, reduce the heat and add half the chives. Simmer for 5 minutes.

For each serving, place one of the pasta sheets on a plate. Scoop 4 scallops with a little sauce onto it. Cover with the other pasta sheet, add 4 more scallops and pour the sauce evenly over the top. Sprinkle the remainder of the cheese over each serving. Mix the pesto with the remaining $1/2$ cup (120 mL) cream and pour it into a squirt bottle (like the ones used for ketchup and mustard at the hot dog stands). Squirt $1/4$ of the pesto on top of each. Place under the broiler to brown the top. Finish with the remaining chives.

Basil Pesto

		MAKES 1 CUP (240 ML)
1 cup	fresh basil, tightly packed	240 mL
1 tsp.	minced garlic	5 mL
1 Tbsp.	pine nuts	15 mL
$1/2$ tsp.	salt	2.5 mL
	pinch black pepper	
$1/4$ cup	Parmesan cheese	60 mL
$1/2$ cup	olive oil	120 mL

Mix everything in a food processor except for the oil. Pulse until it's well mixed, but not too fine. Slowly add the oil until it's all mixed in. Pesto will keep in the fridge for at least 2 weeks, or you can freeze it in ice-cube trays.

PREPARING SCALLOPS

Scallops differ from their mollusk cousins because their shells never close completely. They are usually shucked immediately after they are harvested and to prevent spoilage, the guts are removed and discarded. What remains is the massive muscle. Once shucked, scallops are never eaten raw. All scallops are sold with their tendon, a white strip of gristle that attaches the muscle to the shell. This should be removed by pulling it off.

FISH AND SEAFOOD

Lunch Dishes

Linguine
with Seafood in a Parmesan Alfredo Sauce

Pasta, fast and filling, is one of the most popular lunch items. A little dollop of butter added just before you remove it from the pan will make this dish a little richer and give it that special shine.

1/4 cup	olive oil or butter	60 mL
1/4 cup	minced onion	60 mL
1 tsp.	minced garlic	5 mL
8 oz.	smoked salmon	225 g
8 oz.	baby shrimp	225 g
8 oz.	smoked black cod	225 g
1 1/2 lbs.	pasta, cooked al dente	680 g
2 cups	vegetable or salmon stock (see page 56 or 57)	475 mL
2 cups	whipping cream	475 mL
1 cup	grated Parmesan cheese	240 mL
1 1/2 tsp.	salt	7.5 mL
2 tsp.	black pepper	10 mL
4 Tbsp.	chopped fresh chives	60 mL

Melt the oil or butter in a heavy pan over medium heat. Sauté the onion and garlic for 1 minute. Stir in the salmon, shrimp, cod and pasta. Add the stock. Simmer for 2 minutes and add the cream. Bring to a boil and add 4 Tbsp. (60 mL) of the cheese, the salt, pepper and half the chives. Simmer until it is the consistency of light cream, about 5 minutes. Divide among 4 bowls and top each serving with the remaining cheese and chives.

Pancetta and Tiger Prawn Sandwich
with Salsa Mayonnaise

With this sandwich you can go either way to finish it—that is, a light salad with a vinaigrette or some curly fries with that famous tomato sauce from Leamington, Ontario (Heinz ketchup).

16	tiger prawns, 26/30 count (see page 119), peeled and deveined (see page 121)	16
8	3-inch (7.5-cm) thin slices pancetta	8
4 Tbsp.	oil	60 mL
8	slices sourdough bread	8
4 Tbsp.	butter	60 mL
1 cup	mesclun greens	240 mL
1/2 cup	Tomato Balsamic Salsa (see page 96)	120 mL
4 Tbsp.	mayonnaise (see page 178)	60 mL

Presoak 8 6-inch (15-cm) bamboo skewers in water for 5 minutes.

Place 2 prawns on a piece of pancetta, fold the edges of the pancetta over the prawns and skewer the bacon onto the prawns. Repeat with the remaining prawns and bacon.

Heat the oil in a frying pan over medium heat. Cook the brochettes bacon side down to render the fat out, so that when you turn them over, the prawns cook in the fat for extra flavor. Cooking time should be about 5 minutes on each side.

Butter the bread and grill over a flame if possible. Don't be afraid to let the butter drip into the fire and cause a little flare, because this adds to the flavor. Divide the mesclun between 4 slices of the bread. Remove the bamboo skewers and put 2 skewers of prawns and bacon on each slice. Combine the salsa and mayonnaise and cover the prawns. Top with a second piece of bread. Cut the sandwich in half.

Black Angus Beef Dip
with a Cheese Buttered Bun au Jus

You don't have to use Black Angus beef—any sliced beef from your favorite deli will do. What makes this beef dip a little special is the cheese butter.

1 recipe	Cheese Butter	1 recipe
4	buns, sliced in half	4
1 lb.	sliced medium-rare Black Angus sirloin	455 g
1 recipe	Beef Jus	1 recipe
1	dill pickle	1
2 Tbsp.	chopped fresh chives	30 mL

Spread the butter on each half of the sliced buns and grill or broil just until the butter starts to brown.

Heating the beef is optional, and there are various ways to do it. We steam ours for about 1 minute in a frying pan with about 2 Tbsp. (30 mL) of the jus and then cover with a lid. To microwave, cover the meat with plastic wrap and give it 2 or 3 30-second bursts to heat it up evenly. Turn the meat over and mix it up between each 30-second burst for more even heating. The one problem of heating up the meat is you are cooking it, so medium-rare meat will be well done by the time you are finished. The only way to get rare beef is to cook the beef a little less, slice it hot out of the oven, or serve it cold or at room temperature. Just make sure your jus is good and hot.

Place the meat in the bun and slice it in half. Serve with a slice of dill pickle, sprinkled with chives. Serve each beef dip with $1/2$ cup (120 mL) jus.

Beef Jus

	MAKES 2 CUPS (475 ML)	
2 cups	Brown Stock (see page 59)	475 mL
$1/2$ cup	red wine	120 mL
$1/4$ cup	water	60 mL
1 Tbsp.	minced garlic	15 mL
	salt and black pepper to taste	

Bring to a boil and simmer for 10 minutes, or until reduced to 2 cups (475 mL).

Cheese Butter

		MAKES 1 CUP (240 ML)
1/4 cup	whipped butter	60 mL
1/4 cup	cream cheese	60 mL
1 Tbsp.	minced garlic	15 mL
1 tsp.	paprika	5 mL
1/2 tsp.	salt	2.5 mL
1 tsp.	black pepper	5 mL
2 Tbsp.	grated Parmesan cheese	30 mL
2 Tbsp.	Brie or Camembert cheese	30 mL
1/4 cup	grated Cheddar cheese	30 mL

Put everything in a food processor and process until smooth.

Ahi Tuna Burger
with Onions and Potato Flying Fish Roe Salad

I adapted this recipe for tuna burger seasoning in an issue of *Bon Appetit*. Flying fish roe are the small, bright orange fish eggs found on California rolls. They come in a few flavors and can be found at any Japanese restaurant or market.

1 lb.	ahi tuna, sushi grade, diced	455 g
1 recipe	Tuna Burger Spice Mix	1 recipe
1/2 cup	oil	120 mL
1 cup	sliced onion	240 mL
1 Tbsp.	minced fresh ginger	15 mL
1/4 cup	soy sauce	60 mL
4	poppy seed kaiser buns	4
4 Tbsp.	butter	60 mL
1 recipe	Potato Flying Fish Roe Salad	1 recipe

Place the tuna and 6 Tbsp. (90 mL) of the spice mix in a mixing bowl. Mix well. Refrigerate for at least 30 minutes. Form the tuna into 4 round patties like hamburgers.

In a heavy sauté pan heat 1/2 of the oil over medium-high heat. Add the onion and ginger and cook until brown. Add the soy sauce and simmer for a minute. Remove the onions and keep warm. Return the pan to the heat and add the remaining oil. Add the tuna burgers and cook for 1 minute. Turn them over and cook 1 more minute.

Slice the buns and butter them. Place a patty on the bottom half of each bun, top with some fried onions and some of the spice mix. Serve each tuna burger with a side of potato salad.

Tuna Burger Spice Mix

		MAKES $1/2$ CUP (120 ML)
$1/4$ cup	chopped parsley	60 mL
$1/4$ cup	extra virgin olive oil	60 mL
1 Tbsp.	sherry vinegar	15 mL
1 Tbsp.	minced garlic	15 mL
$1/2$ tsp.	black pepper	2.5 mL
$1/4$ tsp.	ground cumin	1.2 mL
$1/2$ tsp.	cayenne pepper	2.5 mL
1 tsp.	salt	5 mL

Mix everything together and refrigerate.

Potato Flying Fish Roe Salad

		MAKES 3 CUPS (720 ML)
2 cups	cooled roasted potatoes	475 mL
4 Tbsp.	minced celery	60 mL
3 Tbsp.	minced onion	45 mL
3 Tbsp.	chopped fresh parsley	45 mL
3 Tbsp.	mayonnaise (see page 178)	45 mL
1 Tbsp.	rice wine vinegar	15 mL
$1/4$ tsp.	salt	1.2 mL
$1/4$ tsp.	black pepper	1.2 mL
1 Tbsp.	soy sauce	15 mL
$1/2$ tsp.	wasabi powder	2.5 mL
2 Tbsp.	flying fish roe	30 mL

Dice the potatoes and add the celery, onion and parsley. Add the mayonnaise, vinegar, salt and pepper and mix well. Mix together the soy sauce and wasabi powder, pour it over the mixture and fold it in. Gently fold in the flying fish roe.

LUNCH DISHES

131

Salmon Melt
with Tartar Sauce and Coleslaw

This is a very popular lunch item. It has everything you look for in comfort food.

4	4-oz. (113-g) skinless, boneless salmon fillets	4
	pinch salt and black pepper	
4 Tbsp.	oil	60 mL
1/2 cup	butter	120 mL
2 Tbsp.	chopped fresh dill	30 mL
1/4 tsp.	black pepper	1.2 mL
1/2	lemon, zest and juice	1/2
4	slices baguette, 1 inch (2.5 cm) thick, sliced diagonally	4
1/2 lb.	Swiss cheese, in 12 thin slices	225 g
1/2 cup	thinly sliced red onion	120 mL
4	sprigs dill	4
4	wedges lemon	4
3/4 cup	Tartar Sauce (see page 186)	180 mL
4	large lettuce leaves	4
1 recipe	Coleslaw	1 recipe

The salmon fillet should be sliced thin and about 4 inches (10 cm) long. Season with salt and pepper. Heat the oil in a frying pan over medium-high heat. Sear the salmon on both sides, for about a minute per side. Remove from the pan and keep warm.

Put the butter and dill in a food processor. Add the pepper, lemon juice and zest. Combine until well mixed.

Butter the baguette with the dill butter. Place the baguette butter side down in the same pan and fry until the butter browns. Remove the baguette slices and place them butter side up on a baking sheet.

Divide the salmon among the baguette slices. Cover the salmon with the slices of Swiss cheese. Top with the red onion. Place under a broiler to melt the cheese and lightly cook the onion. Place each baguette slice on a plate and top with a sprig of dill. Serve with a lemon wedge and the tartar sauce on the side. Place the coleslaw in a leaf of lettuce to stop the dressing from running.

Coleslaw

2 cups	shredded green cabbage	475 mL
1/4 cup	grated carrot	60 mL
2 Tbsp.	grated onion	30 mL
2 Tbsp.	apple cider	30 mL
1 tsp.	sugar	5 mL
1/4 tsp.	dry mustard	1.2 mL
1/4 tsp.	salt	1.2 mL
2 Tbsp.	minced fresh ginger	30 mL
1 Tbsp.	vegetable oil	15 mL

Combine the cabbage, carrot and onion in a bowl. Whisk the cider, sugar, mustard, salt and ginger together. Pour over the cabbage mixture and toss. Add the oil and mix again.

Focaccia Sandwich
with Roasted Red Peppers and Balsamic Mushrooms

Focaccia is an Italian-style bread that comes in many shapes and sizes. For this recipe I use small round loaves and fill them with everything in the kitchen. This is not a sandwich that is served with a spot of tea—enjoy it with large glass of milk!

2 Tbsp.	balsamic vinegar	30 mL
8	thin slices tomato	8
4	4-inch (10-cm) round focaccia	4
4 Tbsp.	butter	60 mL
4 Tbsp.	olive oil	60 mL
8	leaves butter lettuce	8
4 Tbsp.	mayonnaise (see page 178)	60 mL
2 oz.	sliced or crumbled white Cheddar cheese	57 g
4 oz.	sliced ham	113 g
2 oz.	sliced mozzarella cheese	57 g
4 oz.	sliced smoked turkey	113 g
2 oz.	sliced Swiss cheese	57 g
	pinch salt and black pepper	
1 recipe	Roasted Red Peppers	1 recipe
1 cup	Balsamic Mushrooms	240 mL

Pour the balsamic vinegar over the tomatoes and marinate for as long as possible, but at least 5 minutes.

Slice the focaccia. For each serving, butter the bottom half and pour the olive oil over the top half. Place the butter lettuce on the bottom half and cover with 1 Tbsp. (15 mL) of the mayonnaise. Place 1/4 of the Cheddar, ham, mozzarella, turkey and Swiss cheese on each serving. Remove the tomatoes from the vinegar and place 2 slices on each sandwich. Season with salt and pepper and finally add the top half of the focaccia.

Slice the sandwich in half. It might need a few long toothpicks to help it stay together. Serve with roasted red peppers and a few balsamic mushrooms on the side.

Roasted Red Peppers

		MAKES 1 CUP (240 ML)
2 lb.	sweet red peppers	900 g
1/4 cup	olive oil	60 mL
1 Tbsp.	minced garlic	15 mL
4	anchovy fillets, minced	4
1/4 tsp.	crushed chilies	1.2 mL
2 tsp.	sugar	10 mL
1/2 tsp.	salt	2.5 mL
1/2 tsp.	black pepper	2.5 mL
1 Tbsp.	chopped fresh basil	15 mL
1	lemon, juiced	1

Preheat the oven to 400°F (200°C).

Toss the peppers in the oil and roast for 30 minutes. Cool, remove the core and seeds and cut the peppers into 1/2-inch (1.2-cm) strips. Combine the peppers with the remaining ingredients in a bowl. Cover with oil and refrigerate. The peppers will keep for 3 days.

Balsamic Mushrooms

		MAKES 1 1/2 CUPS (360 ML)
1/4 cup	olive oil	60 mL
1/4 cup	chopped green onions	60 mL
1 Tbsp.	minced garlic	15 mL
1/2 tsp.	salt	2.5 mL
1/2 tsp.	black pepper	2.5 mL
1/2 tsp.	crushed chilies	2.5 mL
2 cups	button mushrooms	475 mL
1 cup	balsamic vinegar	240 mL

Heat the oil in a sauté pan over medium-high heat and sauté the onions, garlic, salt, pepper, chilies and mushrooms for 5 minutes. Add the vinegar and continue cooking until the vinegar is reduced to 1/4 cup (60 mL) and the mushrooms are coated with a thick syrup. Cool and keep in the refrigerator until needed. Leftovers will keep for 2 weeks.

Side Dishes

Aldermeister Potatoes

This goes well with smoked salmon. I peel these new potatoes because the skin usually falls off, but you can leave the skin on if you want.

2 lbs.	new potatoes	900 g
1/4 cup	oil	60 mL
1 cup	sliced onions	240 mL
3 Tbsp.	minced garlic	45 mL
1 tsp.	salt	5 mL
1 Tbsp.	black pepper	15 mL
2 Tbsp.	chopped fresh parsley	30 mL
2 Tbsp.	chopped fresh chives	30 mL
4 Tbsp.	butter	60 mL
4	sprigs parsley	4

Peel the potatoes and slice them into rounds 1/4-inch (.6-cm) thick. Bring a large pot of salted water to a boil and add the potatoes. Return the water to a boil and cook the potatoes for 2 minutes. Drain them well and set aside.

Heat the oil in a 14-inch (36-cm) frying pan over medium-high heat. When the oil begins to smoke, add the potatoes. When they are brown, flip them over and add the onion and garlic. Cook until the onions and potatoes are brown.

Pour off any excess oil. Add the salt, pepper, parsley and chives. Toss and add the butter. Remove from the heat and pack the mixture into 4 6-oz. (170-mL) ramekins or coffee cups. Tap it out onto a plate and garnish each serving with a sprig of parsley.

Scalloped Potatoes

Scalloped potatoes are a great alternative to rice. At the Salmon House we serve them with a variety of grilled seafood.

4 cups	thinly sliced potato, peeled or unpeeled	1 L
1/4 cup	oil	60 mL
2 cups	sliced onion	475 mL
1/4 cup	flour	60 mL
1 tsp.	salt	5 mL
1 tsp.	black pepper	5 mL
1/2 tsp.	nutmeg	2.5 mL
2 cups	grated Parmesan cheese	475 mL
1 tsp.	minced garlic	5 mL
3 cups	whole milk	720 mL

Preheat the oven to 400°F (200°C).

Cover the sliced raw potatoes in water until needed to prevent browning. Heat the oil over medium-high heat and sauté the onion until slightly brown. Set aside. Butter a 12-cup (3-L) casserole dish. Sift the flour, salt, pepper and nutmeg together in a bowl. Drain the potatoes and pat them dry. Place a layer of potato in the baking dish, then some onion. Sprinkle with a little of the flour mixture and add a layer of cheese. Continue this process until the ingredients are used up.

Mix the garlic into the milk and pour it over the potatoes. Do not fill over the top of the potatoes. Place in the oven and reduce the heat to 350°F (175°C). Bake for 50 to 60 minutes. Remove from the oven and let sit for 15 minutes before serving.

SIDE DISHES

Potato Cannelloni

This may sound boring—why would anyone pay for cannelloni filled with potato rather than crab? Well, we do it and it is a popular dish. It pairs well with Pan Roasted Halibut with Almond Dill Pesto (page 111).

4	4 x 4-inch (10 x 10-cm) pasta squares	4
1 lb.	potatoes, peeled and diced	455 g
2 Tbsp.	butter	30 mL
1/4 cup	whole milk	60 mL
	pinch salt and black pepper	
2 cups	oil	475 mL
1/2 cup	thinly sliced onion	120 mL
1 Tbsp.	cornstarch	15 mL

Bring a large pot of water to a boil. Add the pasta squares to the boiling water and salt liberally. Cook, stirring occasionally, until the pasta is tender but still firm to the bite, about 5 minutes. Remove and pat dry.

Cover the diced potatoes with salted water and simmer for 20 minutes. They should be very tender. Drain, add the butter, milk, salt and pepper, and mash.

Heat the oil to 350°F (175°C). Dust the onions with cornstarch and fry until crisp.

Preheat the oven to 350°F (175°C). Fold the onion into the mashed potatoes. Divide the potato among the pasta squares, placing the potato horizontally in the center of the pasta. Roll up the squares and place them seam side down on a baking sheet. Bake for 10 to 15 minutes.

Potato Crêpes

Try these crêpes with smoked salmon or caviar and sour cream.

2 cups	potato, peeled and coarsely grated	475 mL
2 Tbsp.	flour	30 mL
2 tsp.	cornstarch	10 mL
1/2 tsp.	salt	2.5 mL
1 tsp.	black pepper	5 mL
1/2 tsp.	nutmeg	2.5 mL
1/2 cup	whole milk	120 mL
2	whole eggs, slightly beaten	2
1	egg white	1
1/2 cup	vegetable oil	120 mL

Rinse the potatoes in cold water and squeeze them dry. Mix the flour, cornstarch, salt, pepper, nutmeg and milk together and stir the mixture into the potatoes. Mix well and let sit for 5 minutes. Add the eggs and mix well.

In a small skillet, heat 2 tsp. (10 mL) of the oil over medium heat. When it's hot, add 1/4 cup (60 mL) of the crêpe mixture. Cook each side for 2 minutes. The crêpes should be brown and crispy. Place on a cookie sheet in a warm oven while you cook the remaining crêpes.

Cheddar Cheese Potatoes

These potatoes were once served all the time at the Salmon House and were one of its trademark dishes.

5	potatoes, peeled	5
1/2 lb.	grated Cheddar cheese	225 g
1	bunch green onions, chopped	1
2 tsp.	salt	10 mL
2 tsp.	black pepper	10 mL

Preheat the oven to 350°F (175°C).

Steam the potatoes for 15 minutes, or until tender. Cool and slice thinly. Layer the ingredients in a deep casserole dish, alternating potatoes, cheese, green onions and seasoning. Bake until the cheese is melted, about 15 minutes.

Roasted Vegetables

Roasting vegetables gives them a nutty flavor; it's a good alternative to sautéing or steaming. We usually serve them with salmon during the winter months.

1 cup	fennel cut into 1-inch (2.5-cm) dice	240 mL
1 cup	peeled beets cut into 1-inch (2.5-cm) dice	240 mL
1 cup	carrot cut into 1-inch (2.5-cm) dice	240 mL
1 cup	peeled white turnip cut into 1-inch (2.5-cm) dice	240 mL
1 cup	peeled parsnip cut into 1-inch (2.5-cm) dice	240 mL
1 cup	onion cut into 1-inch (2.5-cm) dice	240 mL
1/4 cup	olive oil	60 mL
1 tsp.	salt	5 mL
1 Tbsp.	black pepper	15 mL
2	sprigs thyme	2

Preheat the oven to 350°F (175°C).

Mix all the ingredients together in a bowl. Spread the vegetables on a roasting pan and roast for 30 to 40 minutes. Stir the vegetables halfway through cooking so they cook evenly. The vegetables can be crowded on the pan when roasting; this also helps prevent burning.

ROASTING VEGETABLES

Vegetables do not have any natural oils, so it's important to toss them in a little oil before roasting so they don't dry out. Preheat the oven to 350°F (175°C). Place the oiled vegetables in a roasting pan in the middle of the oven. Roast for about 30 minutes, turning them midway through the cooking time.

SIDE DISHES

Sea Asparagus

Sea asparagus is found on the West Coast of British Columbia and is harvested from May to July. It is salty and has a vivid green color. It does have a tendency to turn black the day after it's cooked, so use it up the same day. You may be able to get it at specialty stores. We get the sea asparagus from Brad "The Seagrass Guy." If you can't find it, use fiddleheads instead.

1 lb.	fresh sea asparagus	455 g
1/2 cup	minced onion	120 mL
4 oz.	unsalted butter	113 g
2 Tbsp.	lemon juice	30 mL

Soak the sea asparagus in cold water for 1 hour, then drain. Bring a large pot of unsalted water to a boil and blanch the sea asparagus for 30 seconds. Plunge it immediately into cold water to cool it down. Drain.

Sauté the onion in the butter for 2 minutes over medium heat. Add the sea asparagus and sauté for 2 minutes. Stir in the lemon juice and serve immediately.

Grilled Chili-Crusted Salmon
with Tomato Balsamic Salsa and
Tortilla Chips (page 103)

Lunch is served at the
Salmon House on the Hill

Salmon House Hot Pot
(page 48)

Alaska Black Cod with Curry, Apple and Carrot Butter and Ginger Couscous (page 114)

Asparagus Glazed
with Orange Hollandaise

I use the thinner (pencil-size) asparagus rather than the larger, woodier ones because they cook more evenly and are milder in taste.

2 lbs.	asparagus, woody ends trimmed off	900 g
3 Tbsp.	minced onion	45 mL
2 Tbsp.	chopped fresh thyme	30 mL
1 Tbsp.	malt vinegar	15 mL
1 tsp.	lemon juice	5 mL
	dash hot pepper sauce	
1 cup	orange juice	240 mL
5	egg yolks	5
3/4 cup	clarified butter (see page 44)	180 mL
	pinch salt and black pepper	

Bring a large pot of water to a boil and add the asparagus. The thickness of the stalks will determine how long you cook it; usually 2 minutes is more than enough. Unless you are going to eat the asparagus right away, place it in ice water to stop the cooking.

Combine the onion, thyme, vinegar, lemon juice, hot pepper sauce and orange juice in a small pot and cook over low heat until it's reduced to 4 Tbsp. (60 mL). Transfer to a double boiler and whisk in the egg yolks. Continue cooking and whisking over simmering water until it's thick. Add the cooled clarified butter slowly to the egg mixture, drop by drop at first, whisking all the time. Season with salt and pepper. Place in a non-reactive container and keep warm.

To serve, place the asparagus in a heatproof serving dish and cover with the hollandaise sauce. Place under a broiler until the hollandaise is brown.

SIDE DISHES

Fiddleheads
with Walnuts and Browned Butter

Fiddleheads are new, tightly coiled (hence the name) fern fronds. Fresh ones are available only in spring. You cook them like asparagus.

1 lb.	fiddleheads, trimmed	455 g
1/2 cup	butter	120 mL
2 Tbsp.	minced onion	30 mL
1 cup	walnuts, halved	240 mL
	pinch salt and black pepper	

Blanch the fiddleheads in salted boiling water for 1 minute. Drain. Place 2 Tbsp. (30 mL) of the butter in a sauté pan over medium heat. Add the onion and walnuts. Toss and add the fiddleheads. Add the rest of the butter, season with salt and pepper and sauté until the fiddleheads are cooked and the butter is browned, about 5 minutes.

Artichoke Fritters

I like serving these with lamb. The globe artichoke is listed as a vegetable, but is really the large bud of a thistle-like plant. The Jerusalem artichoke is a tuber.

10	canned artichokes, drained, cut in half	10
1	lemon, juiced	1
1/2 tsp.	salt	2.5 mL
1/2 tsp.	black pepper	2.5 mL
2	eggs, slightly beaten	2
2/3 cup	flour	160 mL
	vegetable oil	

Place the artichokes in a large bowl, pour the lemon juice over them and toss. Add the salt and pepper. Mix the eggs into the artichokes. Let sit for 5 minutes. Place the flour in a bowl. Strain the artichokes and toss them in the flour. Heat 2 inches (5 cm) of oil in a wide, 8- to 9-quart (8- to 9-L) pot over moderately high heat until the deep-fat thermometer registers 350°F (175°C). Add the artichokes and fry for 5 minutes. Remove and drain on a paper towel. Serve immediately.

Conch and Cheese Fritters

A conch is a tropical mollusk with a large, often brightly colored spiral shell and edible flesh. You will find conch meat in the frozen exotic seafood section of the supermarket.

6 Tbsp.	flour	90 mL
1/2 tsp.	salt	2.5 mL
1/2 tsp.	cayenne pepper	2.5 mL
1/2 tsp.	black pepper	2.5 mL
1 tsp.	baking powder	5 mL
1/2 tsp.	baking soda	2.5 mL
3 Tbsp.	whole milk	45 mL
3 Tbsp.	water, approximately	45 mL
1 cup	minced conch	240 mL
1/4 cup	grated aged Cheddar cheese	60 mL
1/4 cup	chopped green onion	60 mL
4	egg whites	4
	vegetable oil for frying	

Combine the flour, salt, cayenne pepper, black pepper, baking powder and baking soda. Add the milk and then enough water to make a stiff batter. Add the conch, cheese and onion and mix well. Whip the egg whites until they form stiff peaks and add them to the mixture.

Heat 2 inches (5 cm) of oil in a wide, 8- to 9-quart (8- to 9-L) pot until the deep-fat thermometer registers 350°F (175°C). Carefully drop the batter in the oil, a heaping tablespoon at a time. (If you dip your spoon in oil before scooping the batter out, the batter will slide off the spoon a little easier.) Cook until golden brown, about 2 to 3 minutes. Turn them over and cook the other side.

Remove the fritters and drain on paper towel.

Risotto

Arborio rice is an Italian short-grain rice. Its high starch content makes it great for risotto. Stirring constantly while adding the stock is the secret to a creamy texture.

6 Tbsp.	unsalted butter	90 mL
1 Tbsp.	olive oil	15 mL
1/2 cup	minced onion	120 mL
2 cups	Arborio rice	475 mL
1 cup	white wine	240 mL
5 cups	chicken stock (see page 57)	1.2 L
	salt and black pepper to taste	
1 cup	grated Parmesan cheese	240 mL

Place half the butter and oil in a heavy saucepan over medium heat. Add the onion and rice and stir for a couple of minutes. Add the white wine and 1 cup (240 mL) of the stock. Bring to a simmer and stir until the liquid is gone. Add 2 more cups (475 mL) of the stock and repeat the process, stirring to make sure the rice doesn't stick to the bottom of the pot. Add the last 2 cups (475 mL) of stock and simmer again to reduce the stock. Stir in the salt, pepper and the remaining 3 Tbsp. (45 mL) of butter. Serve with the Parmesan cheese on top.

Bannock Bread

Bannock is a great substitute for yeast bread. It is delicious with jam, butter or molasses.

3 cups	unbleached flour, approximately	720 mL
1 Tbsp.	baking powder	15 mL
1 tsp.	salt	5 mL
1 1/2 cups	warm milk	360 mL
	vegetable oil	

Combine the flour, baking powder and salt. Add the warm milk and knead until the dough is soft and smooth. At the Salmon House we usually need a little more flour. Do not overwork the dough. Form the dough into a ball, brush it with a little oil, and let rest for 1 hour.

Roll out the dough to an inch (2.5 cm) thick and cut it into 2-inch (5-cm) triangles or squares. Heat 2 inches (5 cm) of oil in a wide, 8- to 9-quart (8- to 9-L) pot over moderately high heat until the deep-fat thermometer registers 350°F (175°C). Cook the bread until it's golden brown, turning it at least once. Drain on a paper towel. Serve immediately.

Spaetzle

Spaetzle is a starch-type dish that can be substituted for potatoes, rice or pasta. It is very versatile and freezes well.

3	whole eggs	3
1 cup	whole milk	240 mL
3 cups	flour	720 mL
2 tsp.	salt	10 mL
1 tsp.	black pepper	5 mL
6 Tbsp.	chopped fresh parsley	90 mL
6 Tbsp.	chopped fresh chives	90 mL

Whisk the eggs and milk together until they're fully combined. Stir in the flour, salt, pepper and herbs. Mix the dough with your hand or a spatula until air pockets form. This is done by repeatedly scooping the dough up and over.

Bring a pot of salted water to a rapid boil. Press the dough through a colander with $1/4$-inch (.6-cm) holes. The bigger the holes, the bigger the spaetzle. Drop the spaetzle into the boiling water and cook for 2 to 5 minutes. The spaetzle should float to the surface when it's done. Drain and serve right away with butter or gravy. It will keep in the refrigerator for 2 to 3 days. To reheat, fry in butter.

Desserts

Mocha Torte

This dessert is a Salmon House specialty.

FOR THE BOTTOM LAYER:

2 1/2 cups	pecan halves	600 mL
1/2 cup	sugar	120 mL
1/2 cup	melted butter	120 mL

Preheat the oven to 350°F (175°C). Line a 10-inch (25-cm) springform pan with silicone or parchment paper.

Coarsely grind the pecans in a food processor. Add the sugar and melted butter and mix well. Press into the prepared pan. Bake for 10 minutes, remove from the oven and cool. There should be no difference in color between the edges and the middle of the crust.

FOR THE SECOND LAYER:

1 cup	whipping cream	240 mL
1/4 lb.	butter	113 g
2 Tbsp.	corn syrup	30 mL
1/2 lb.	unsweetened dark chocolate	225 g

Combine the cream, butter and corn syrup in a saucepan. Bring to a boil and pour it over the chocolate. Stir until the chocolate is melted, stirring in one direction if possible. This will create a nice shine and even mixing. Cool the mixture to room temperature before pouring it over the crust. Depending on how cool it is, you might have to smooth this layer with a spatula. Put the pan in the fridge to chill.

FOR THE THIRD LAYER:

6 1/2 oz.	Callebaut chocolate or other chocolate	182 g
1 Tbsp.	gelatin powder	15 mL
4 Tbsp.	cold water	60 mL
1/3 cup	Demerara sugar	80 mL
2 Tbsp.	espresso	30 mL
3 cups	whipping cream	720 mL

Gently melt the chocolate in a bowl or double boiler over simmering water. I usually cover the container holding the chocolate with plastic wrap to keep the chocolate warm. Soften the gelatin in the water for about 10 minutes. Place the softened gelatin, sugar and espresso in a small pot and melt over low heat. Combine with the melted chocolate and stir until mixed. Whip the cream. Stir in about $^1/_5$ of the cream into the chocolate mixture. Fold in the rest of the whipped cream with a spatula. Pour the mixture over the second layer. Smooth and level the top. Freeze the torte.

FOR THE FOURTH LAYER:

2 Tbsp.	sugar	30 mL
1 tsp.	cocoa powder	5 mL
2 cups	whipping cream	475 mL

Sift the sugar and cocoa into the cream and whip until stiff. Remove the torte from the freezer and spread the whipped cream around the sides and on top of the torte. (Freezing makes it easier to put the fourth layer on, as it keeps it firm.) A few coffee beans or chocolate coffee beans on top is a nice touch. Thaw in the refrigerator—about 1 hour—before serving.

Turtle Pie

We thought this dessert had the texture and flavor of those incredible little chocolates called Turtles. We serve it with a slice of vanilla ice cream.

FOR THE CRUST:

1 1/2 cups	flour	360 mL
1/4 tsp.	salt	1.2 mL
1/4 tsp.	baking powder	1.2 mL
3 Tbsp.	sugar	45 mL
1	egg	1
6 Tbsp.	cold unsalted butter	90 mL
2–3 Tbsp.	cold water	30–45 mL

Place the flour, salt, baking powder and sugar in a food processor and pulse 10 times. Add the egg and pulse 10 times. Add the butter and water and pulse 20 times. The dough should come away from the sides of the bowl. Roll it out and press it into a 10-inch (25-cm) tart pan.

FOR THE FILLING:

1 cup	unsalted butter	240 mL
1/4 cup	honey	60 mL
1/4 cup	granulated sugar	60 mL
1 cup	Demerara sugar	240 mL
1/4 cup	whipping cream	60 mL
2 cups	pecans	475 mL

Preheat the oven to 325°F (165°C).

Place the butter, honey, and sugars in a saucepan and bring to a boil, stirring constantly. Boil for 3 minutes. Remove from the heat and add the cream and pecans. Pour the mixture into the crust and bake for 30 minutes. Cool to room temperature.

FOR THE GANACHE:

1/2 cup	whipping cream	120 mL
2 Tbsp.	unsalted butter	30 mL
2 Tbsp.	sugar	30 mL
12 oz.	dark chocolate, grated	340 g
2 oz.	white chocolate	57 g

Place the cream, butter and sugar in a heavy pot over medium-high heat. Bring it to a boil. Make sure the sugar is dissolved. Pour the mixture over the dark chocolate. Stir in one direction until the chocolate has melted and the mixture is smooth. Pour the mixture over the cooled filling. Level it off so it's smooth and flat.

Melt the white chocolate over hot water. Pour the chocolate into a piping bag with a narrow tip. Pipe straight lines 3/4 inch (1.9 cm) apart over the top of the pie.

Drag a bamboo skewer across the lines of white chocolate, making a wave effect. Refrigerate until serving time.

White and Dark Chocolate Mousse Pie

This dessert freezes well and is even good frozen, although I prefer it at refrigerator temperature. Serve it with a dollop of whipped cream and a strawberry.

FOR THE CRUST:

2 cups	Oreo cookie crumbs or other cookie crumbs	475 mL
2/3 cup	clarified butter (see page 44)	160 mL

Line the bottom of a 10-inch (25-cm) springform pan with silicone paper. If you don't use silicone paper, brush the pan with butter and then dust with flour. Mix the butter and cookie crumbs together and press the mixture onto the bottom of the pan. Place in the refrigerator to chill.

FOR THE DARK CHOCOLATE LAYER:

5 1/3 oz.	unsweetened dark chocolate	150 g
3	egg yolks	3
2 Tbsp.	sugar	30 mL
1 cup	whipping cream	240 mL

The dark chocolate is best for the bottom layer because the white chocolate tends to be a little softer. Melt the chocolate in a bowl over hot water and stir until smooth. Cover with plastic wrap and keep warm. Beat the egg yolks with the sugar until the mixture thickens, about 10 minutes. Combine the egg and chocolate. Whip the cream and fold it into the chocolate mixture. Spoon onto the crust and make it as level as possible. Refrigerate.

FOR THE WHITE CHOCOLATE LAYER:

5 1/3 oz.	white chocolate	150 g
3	egg yolks	3
2 Tbsp.	sugar	30 mL
1 cup	whipping cream	240 mL

Melt the white chocolate in a bowl over hot water and stir until smooth. Cover with plastic wrap and keep warm. Beat the egg yolks with sugar until they thicken, about 10 minutes. Combine the egg and chocolate.

Whip the cream and fold it into the white chocolate mixture. Spoon the white chocolate mixture over the dark chocolate layer, making it as level as possible. Refrigerate for 24 hours. Cut into wedges.

Chocolate Mousse

At a chocolate seminar I learned 6 or 7 methods of making chocolate mousse. Here is one way to make this delectable concoction. We serve it in a parfait glass with a strawberry and a little icing sugar.

4 Tbsp.	butter	60 mL
8 oz.	unsweetened dark chocolate, grated	225 g
4	eggs, separated	4
1 Tbsp.	cold water	15 mL
1 Tbsp.	Crème de Cacao or other coffee liqueur	15 mL
2 cups	whipping cream	475 mL

Melt the butter in the top of a double boiler over hot water. Add the chocolate and stir until it's melted. Place the egg yolks, water and crème de cacao in a bowl or pot over hot water and beat until thick, about 10 minutes.

Beat the egg whites until they form stiff peaks. Fold into the chocolate. Whip the cream and fold it into the chocolate mixture. Refrigerate for 24 hours before serving in individual glasses.

DESSERTS

159

Blueberry Pie

I grew up on blueberry crisp and the Salmon House grew up on blueberry cobbler. We had to meet somewhere. This simple dessert falls into the category of comfort food and is a big hit whenever we serve it. Serve it with ice cream, whipped cream or just by itself, warm from the oven.

FOR THE PASTRY:

2 cups	flour	475 mL
1/2 tsp.	salt	2.5 mL
1 Tbsp.	sugar	15 mL
1/4 cup	butter	60 mL
1/4 cup	lard	60 mL
5 Tbsp.	cold water	75 mL

Combine the flour, salt and sugar in a bowl. Grate the butter and lard into the flour. Sprinkle the water over the top and mix lightly until the dough comes together in a ball. Cover with plastic wrap and chill for 30 minutes. Divide the dough in two. On a lightly floured surface, roll 1 piece out to 1/4 inch (.6 cm) thick. Fit it into a pie plate, flute the edges and chill again until firm.

FOR THE FILLING:

1/2 cup	sugar	120 mL
2 Tbsp.	flour	30 mL
1	orange, zest only	1
2 Tbsp.	cornstarch	30 mL
4 cups	blueberries	1 L
2 Tbsp.	butter	30 mL

Mix the sugar, flour, zest and cornstarch in a bowl. Add the blueberries and mix well. Place in the pie shell and dot with the butter.

TO FINISH THE PIE:

1	whole egg, slightly beaten	1
2 Tbsp.	sugar	30 mL

Preheat the oven to 350°F (175°C).

Roll out the remaining dough. Brush the rim of the bottom crust with the egg and place the top over the filling. Pinch the top and bottom edges together. Brush the top with egg and sprinkle with sugar. Cut a hole in the top for steam to escape. Bake for 30 to 40 minutes, until the top is browned and the juices are bubbling.

Fresh Fruit Salsa
with Balsamic Vinegar and Black Pepper

Fresh fruit and balsamic vinegar could go equally well on a salad or with ice cream. Now you can say you have tried everything.

1 cup	balsamic vinegar	240 mL
1 Tbsp.	lemon juice	15 mL
1/2 cup	honey	120 mL
2 Tbsp.	cracked black pepper	30 mL
1 cup	strawberries, hulled and quartered	240 mL
1 cup	blueberries	240 mL
1 cup	pineapple, pared and diced	240 mL
1 cup	mango, peeled, seeded and diced	240 mL
1 cup	kiwi, peeled and diced	240 mL
4	sprigs mint	4

Place the vinegar, lemon juice, honey and pepper in a bowl and mix well. Add the fruit and toss. Cover and refrigerate for 1 hour. Divide the salsa between 4 sundae glasses. Serve with a sprig of mint.

DESSERTS

Pear and Rum Charlotte
with Fruit Purées

This is an old recipe adapted from the classic charlotte russe. It has an incredible light texture and always tastes like more. The strawberry jelly rolls are available in grocery stores. We use Austrian rum for its unique flavor.

2	packages strawberry jelly rolls	2
3 Tbsp.	unsalted butter	45 mL
1 Tbsp.	gelatin powder	15 mL
4 Tbsp.	water	60 mL
1	10-oz. (284-mL) can pears in syrup	1
6	whole eggs	6
$2/3$ cup	sugar	160 mL
1 $1/3$ cups	whole milk	320 mL
3 Tbsp.	Austrian dark rum or other rum	45 mL
1 $1/3$ cups	whipping cream	320 mL
1 recipe	Fruit Purées	1 recipe

Cut the jelly rolls into $1/4$-inch (.6-cm) slices. Butter the bottom and sides of a 7-cup (1.7 L) metal bowl. Line the bottom and sides with the jelly roll slices. If there are any slices left, you can put them on top of the charlotte while it sets.

Dissolve the gelatin in the water. Drain the pears and cut them into $1/2$-inch (1.2-cm) cubes.

Combine the eggs, sugar and milk in a mixing bowl. Beat slightly. Place the bowl over simmering water on medium heat and whisk the mixture until it's double in volume and very thick. It should take about 10 minutes.

Warm the gelatin and water mixture over low heat. Strain the melted gelatin into the egg and milk mixture. Place the hot mixture over a bowl of ice and continue to whisk. Add the rum and continue to whisk until the mixture is slightly cooler than room temperature.

Whip the cream and fold it into the mixture. Pour into the lined bowl. Drop the diced pears into the mixture, trying to distribute them evenly. Chill for 24 hours.

To remove the charlotte, have a serving plate ready. Fill your sink up with very hot water. Dip the blade of a very thin paring knife into the water and run the blade around the inside top 1 inch (2.5 cm) of the bowl. This will give the charlotte a head start when coming out of the mold. Holding the bowl by the lip, place it in the water to within an inch (2.5 cm) of the top for 30 to 60 seconds. Place the plate over top of the bowl and invert the charlotte onto the plate. Give it a little shake and the charlotte will come out nicely. Refrigerate again for 30 minutes.

To serve, cut the charlotte into wedges, using a long thin blade dipped in hot water. Serve with 2 Tbsp. (30 mL) of each fruit purée.

Fruit Purées

	MAKES 3/4 CUP (180 ML)	
1/2 cup	fresh blueberries	120 mL
1/2 cup	fresh strawberries	120 mL
1/2 cup	fresh ripe mango, peeled and stone removed	120 mL
3/4 cup	simple syrup (see page 169)	180 mL

In a blender, purée each fruit separately with 1/4 cup (60 mL) of the syrup. Refrigerate in separate bowls until needed.

Blood Orange Chiffon Cake

I have always loved the name of this cake. I use blood oranges not because of the flavor, but more for the bright color and the name.

2 1/2 cups	cake flour	600 mL
1 1/2 cups	sugar	360 mL
2 tsp.	baking powder	10 mL
1/2 tsp.	baking soda	2.5 mL
1/2 tsp.	salt	2.5 mL
1/2 cup	vegetable oil	120 mL
5	egg yolks	5
3/4 cup	freshly squeezed blood orange juice	180 mL
1 Tbsp.	grated blood orange peel	15 mL
1 cup	egg whites	240 mL
1/2 tsp.	cream of tartar	2.5 mL
3/4 cup	icing sugar	180 mL
4 Tbsp.	blood orange juice	60 mL

Preheat the oven to 350°F (175°C).

Combine the flour, sugar, baking powder, baking soda and salt in a bowl. Mix the vegetable oil and egg yolks together, make a well in the flour mixture and pour in the liquid mixture. Add the 3/4 cup (180 mL) orange juice and the zest and blend with a wooden spoon.

In a separate bowl, combine the egg whites and cream of tartar and beat until stiff peaks form. Fold into the flour mixture. Pour into a 10-inch (25-cm) ungreased tube pan with a removable bottom. Bake in the center of the oven for 55 minutes. Lower the heat to 325°F (165°C) and bake for another 10 minutes. Remove the cake and immediately invert it on a rack. Let the cake cool completely upside-down in the pan.

Remove the cake from the pan and place it on a serving platter. Combine the icing sugar and the 4 Tbsp. (60 mL) orange juice. Drizzle over the cake.

DESSERTS

Green Tea Tiramisu

I enjoy a nice cup of green tea, and when I tasted the refreshing Sobe green tea it gave me this idea. Unlike the Italian classic, this is not made with mascarpone cheese. Look for Vicenzovo ladyfingers.

4	bottles Sobe green tea	4
30	^{1}/2-oz. (14-g) green tea bags	30
2	drops green food coloring	2
1	14-oz. (400-g) package ladyfingers	1
2 cups	cream cheese	475 mL
1 cup	icing sugar	240 mL
^{1}/2 cup	sour cream	120 mL
1 Tbsp.	minced fresh ginger	15 mL

Combine the bottled Sobe and the tea bags in a pot, bring to a simmer, and remove from the heat. Let sit for 30 minutes. Strain, squeezing out all the liquid. Measure out 1 cup (240 mL) and add the 2 drops of food coloring. Cook over medium heat until it's reduced to ^{1}/4 cup (60 mL). Set aside to cool.

Line a 10-inch (25-cm) springform pan with clear plastic wrap. Cut the ladyfingers so they stand about ^{1}/4 inch (.6 cm) above the rim of the pan. Dip them into the green tea mix without the food coloring and line the outside of the pan, cut side down. Line the bottom of the pan with ladyfingers dipped in tea. You will have to cut them to the shape you need to cover the bottom of the pan.

Blend the cream cheese in a food processor until smooth. Add the icing sugar and mix again. Gradually add the sour cream and ginger. Add the ^{1}/4 cup (60 mL) of green tea mixed with food coloring and mix until smooth. Pour ^{1}/2 of the cream cheese mixture into the pan and cover with another layer of ladyfingers dipped in tea. Top this layer with the rest of the cream cheese mix. Refrigerate and let set overnight.

Remove the sides of the springform pan, cut into 12 portions and remove each portion with a spatula.

Norwegian Omelette (Baked Alaska)

The egg whites for the meringue in this recipe should be cold and absolutely yolk-free. I found out the hard way that if there is anything that will stop egg whites from whipping up it is any kind of fat (such as the yolk) or heat. Even a plastic bowl can retain fats and oils. The best type of bowl is a copper bowl because it helps the egg white to stay fluffy.

FOR THE CAKE:

1/2 lb.	butter, room temperature	225 g
2 cups	sugar	475 mL
4	eggs, room temperature	4
4 oz.	semi-sweet chocolate	113 g
2 tsp.	vanilla	10 mL
3 cups	all-purpose flour	720 mL
1/2 tsp.	salt	2.5 mL
1/2 tsp.	baking soda	2.5 mL
1 cup	buttermilk	240 mL

Preheat the oven to 350°F (175°C). Grease a 10-inch (25-cm) square cake pan lightly and dust it with flour.

Cream the butter and sugar together in a kitchen machine with paddle attachment or a hand mixer. Add the eggs 1 at a time, beating well after each addition. Melt the chocolate in a bowl placed over hot water. Combine the vanilla and melted chocolate and fold into the creamed mixture with a spatula.

Sift the flour, salt and baking soda together. Add the flour mixture and the buttermilk alternately to the creamed mixture. Mix well after each addition. Scrape down the bowl as the ingredients are added. Pour the batter into the prepared pan and bake for 1 hour and 20 minutes. Cool before removing from the pan.

FOR THE MERINGUE:

6	egg whites	6
1 cup	sugar	240 mL
$1/4$ cup	Grand Marnier or other orange liqueur	60 mL

Combine the egg whites and sugar in a kitchen machine with the whip attachment or hand mixer. Start with a slow speed, then after about 1 minute, whip on high speed for about 10 minutes. The meringue should be thick and smooth. Fold in the Grand Marnier. You should have about 4 cups (1 L).

TO ASSEMBLE:

$1/4$ cup	Grand Marnier or other orange liqueur	60 mL
3 cups	cherry ice cream	720 mL
$1/4$ cup	unsalted, blanched pistachios	60 mL
$1/4$ cup	icing sugar	60 mL
	fresh cherries	

Preheat the oven to 450°F (230°C). Slice the cake in half horizontally. Pour the Grand Marnier on the bottom half and spread the ice cream over it. Cover with the top half of the cake. Put the cake on an ovenproof dish. Cover with the meringue and gently place the nuts on the cake. Sprinkle with icing sugar and bake for 5 to 7 minutes, or until golden brown. Garnish with a few fresh cherries and more icing sugar. Show it off before you slice it up. I prefer not to freeze it before baking so the cake is not frozen when you eat it.

Crêpe Fettucini
with Peach Balls and Raspberry Sauce

The recipe calls for ice cream, sorbet or fresh peaches, but there's no reason you couldn't put all three on the crêpes. Either or all will work fine. This recipe makes 24 crêpes but you'll only need 8 for the dish. You can refrigerate the batter for 2 or 3 days or cook all the crêpes and freeze them. They freeze well and take no time at all to defrost.

2 Tbsp.	sugar	30 mL
1 1/4 cups	all-purpose flour	300 mL
	pinch salt	
4	eggs	4
2 cups	homogenized milk	475 mL
2 Tbsp.	vanilla	30 mL
2 Tbsp.	Grand Marnier or other orange liqueur	30 mL
1/4 cup	vegetable oil	60 mL
4 tsp.	sugar	20 mL
1/4 cup	simple syrup (see page 169)	60 mL
1/2 cup	raspberries	120 mL
20–24	peach balls	20–24
4 Tbsp.	icing sugar	60 mL
4	sprigs mint	4

To make the batter, sift the sugar, flour and salt together. Place the eggs, milk, vanilla, Grand Marnier and 1 Tbsp. (15 mL) vegetable oil in a blender. Add the dry ingredients. Purée for 30 seconds, scrape down the sides and purée for 30 more seconds. Strain and let sit 20 to 30 minutes before cooking, for best results.

Place about 1 tsp. (5 mL) oil on a 10-inch (25-cm) non-stick pan over medium heat. Add 3 Tbsp. (45 mL) crêpe batter and cook for 1 minute. Turn the crêpe over and cook for another minute. You will need 8 crêpes.

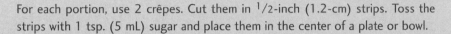

For each portion, use 2 crêpes. Cut them in $^1/_2$-inch (1.2-cm) strips. Toss the strips with 1 tsp. (5 mL) sugar and place them in the center of a plate or bowl.

To make the raspberry sauce, pour the syrup into a blender, add the raspberries and purée until smooth. Strain and set aside.

For the peach balls you can use peach ice cream, peach sorbet or fresh peaches. To make the balls, use a 1 tsp. (5 mL) melon baller, or an even smaller one for a different effect if you use fresh peaches. Place 5 to 6 peach balls over the crêpe strips and top with the raspberry purée. Finish with a dusting of icing sugar and a sprig of fresh mint.

SIMPLE SYRUP

Simple syrup is a mixture of sugar and water, usually equal parts by volume. The mix is brought to a boil and simmered for 5 minutes to dissolve the sugar. The mixture is kept in the fridge until needed. It will keep for a long time. If the sugar crystallizes, bring it back to a simmer to melt the sugar again.

Peach Crisp
with Southern Comfort Ice Cream

The crisp is classic comfort food. Peaches are good for crisps because you can use canned, fresh or frozen slices.

8 cups	sliced peaches	2 L
1 cup	granulated sugar	240 mL
3 Tbsp.	all-purpose flour	45 mL
2 tsp.	cinnamon	10 mL
$^1/_2$ cup	fresh orange juice with pulp	120 mL
2 cups	all-purpose flour	475 mL
2 cups	rolled oats	475 mL
1 $^1/_2$ cups	Demerara sugar	360 mL
1 tsp.	grated orange zest	5 mL
1 cup	melted butter	240 mL
2 cups	Southern Comfort Ice Cream	475 mL

Preheat the oven to 350°F (175°C). Butter a 11 x 16-inch (28 x 40-cm) baking dish.

Combine the peaches, granulated sugar, 3 Tbsp. (45 mL) flour, cinnamon and orange juice in a bowl and mix well. Place in the prepared baking dish.

Mix the 2 cups (475 mL) flour, rolled oats, Demerara sugar and zest in a bowl. Pour the melted butter over the mixture. Mix well, until the mixture forms pea-sized crumbs. Spread the crumbs evenly over the peach mixture.

Bake for 50 to 60 minutes, until the top is browned and the peach juices are bubbling. Serve hot, topped with a scoop of ice cream.

Southern Comfort Ice Cream

		MAKES 6 CUPS (1.5 L)
2 cups	whole milk	475 mL
2 cups	half-and-half cream	475 mL
1 cup	whipping cream	240 mL
3/4 cup	sugar	180 mL
3	large eggs	3
3	large egg yolks	3
1 tsp.	vanilla	5 mL
2 Tbsp.	honey	30 mL
1/4 cup	Southern Comfort or other whiskey liqueur	60 mL

Combine the milk, cream and sugar in a saucepan. Place over medium heat and bring the mixture almost to a boil. Lightly beat the eggs, yolks and vanilla together. Mix a little of the scalded cream mixture into the egg mixture to temper the eggs. Combine the egg mixture and the scalded mixture and whisk until smooth.

Place over medium-high heat and cook and stir with a spatula until the temperature reaches 180°F (82°C). Turn the heat to low and carefully cook and stir for 10 minutes. Remove from the heat and add the honey and Southern Comfort. Strain through a sieve. Cool and refrigerate overnight. Freeze in an ice cream machine according to the manufacturer's instructions.

Apple Strudel
with Cheddar Cheese Ice Cream

Apple and cheese complement each other very well in this recipe.

1/4 cup	butter	60 mL
1 cup	bread crumbs	240 mL
1 lb.	frozen puff pastry, thawed	455 g
6 cups	peeled tart apples, core removed, diced	1.5 L
2 cups	Demerara sugar	475 mL
4 Tbsp.	lemon zest	60 mL
4 Tbsp.	cinnamon	60 mL
1/3 cup	cold butter, broken into pea-size pieces	80 mL
1	egg, lightly beaten	1
2 Tbsp.	granulated sugar	30 mL
1/4 cup	icing sugar	60 mL
4 cups	vanilla ice cream	1 L
1 cup	grated Cheddar cheese	240 mL

Preheat the oven to 400°F (200°C).

In a large flat frying pan over medium heat, melt the 1/4 cup (60 mL) butter. Add the bread crumbs and sauté for 4 to 5 minutes, until golden brown. Cool.

On a lightly floured surface, roll the puff pastry out as thin as possible to less than 1/4 inch (.6 cm), into a rectangle about 16 x 24 inches (40 x 60 cm). Leaving a 2-inch (5-cm) border, sprinkle the bread crumbs over the dough. Repeat with the apples, Demerara sugar, lemon zest, cinnamon and butter.

Roll the strudel up like a jelly roll and place it on a cookie sheet, seam side down. Tuck in the outside edges. If you don't have a 24-inch (60-cm) cookie sheet, you can shape the strudel into an S, V or N. Brush with egg and sprinkle with the sugar.

Bake for 10 minutes, then reduce the heat to 350°F (175°C) and bake for another 30 minutes. Remove from the oven and dust heavily with icing sugar.

Heat up an old knife until it is red hot. Mark the strudel with criss-crossing lines. Be careful—there will be a puff of steam each time you touch the sugar with the knife.

Soften the ice cream. Mix in the cheese and refreeze. Cut a slice of the strudel while it is still warm and serve with a scoop of the ice cream.

Sun-Dried Cherry Scones

Scones are quick breads, which can be substituted for cakes in many recipes, such as strawberry shortcake.

2 2/3 cups	flour	635 mL
1/3 cup	sugar	80 mL
1 1/2 tsp.	baking powder	22.5 mL
1 tsp.	baking soda	5 mL
1 tsp.	salt	5 mL
1/2 cup	diced cold unsalted butter plus 2 Tbsp.	150 mL
2 cups	sun-dried cherries	475 mL
2 2/3 cups	rolled oats	635 mL
1 1/3 cups	buttermilk	320 mL
1	large egg	1

Preheat the oven to 400°F (200°C). Line two 12 x 18-inch (30 x 46-cm) baking sheets with parchment paper, or grease the pans.

Place the flour, sugar, baking powder, baking soda and salt in a food processor and process until just combined. With the motor still running, add the butter and process until the mixture looks like coarse meal. Transfer to a bowl and mix in the cherries and rolled oats.

Place the buttermilk and egg in a small bowl and mix thoroughly with a whisk. Remove 1/4 cup (60 mL) of this mixture and set it aside. Pour the remaining mixture over the dry ingredients and lightly stir everything together, just until it is evenly moistened. Using your hands, drop the dough in mounds about 4 inches (10 cm) in diameter onto the prepared baking sheets. Using a pastry brush, dab the reserved buttermilk and egg mixture over the tops of the scones. Bake for 2 minutes, then reduce the oven temperature to 375°F (190°C) and bake for 10 to 15 minutes longer. Remove and cool on a wire rack.

Cinnamon Rolls
with Kahlua Icing

Hot out of the oven, covered with Kahlua icing, a cinnamon roll goes very well with an after-dinner coffee or tea.

2 cups	hot water	475 mL
1 cup	whole milk	240 mL
1/3 cup	sugar	80 mL
1	egg	1
3 Tbsp.	instant yeast	45 mL
7–8 cups	all-purpose flour	1.7–2 L
1/3 cup	margarine, melted	80 mL
2 tsp.	salt	10 mL
1/3 cup	melted butter	80 mL
3/4 cup	Demerara sugar	180 mL
3/4 cup	granulated sugar	180 mL
3 Tbsp.	cinnamon	45 mL
1 tsp.	cocoa powder	5 mL
1 cup	icing sugar	240 mL
4 Tbsp.	Kahlua or other coffee liqueur	60 mL

In a very large bowl combine the hot water and milk. The mixture should be luke-warm. Add the sugar, egg and yeast. Whisk until smooth. Add 3 cups (720 mL) of the flour and mix until smooth. Add the melted margarine and salt, and beat until well mixed. Add another 3 1/2 cups (840 mL) of the flour and stir with a wooden spoon until mixed together. Knead in the last 1/2 cup (120 mL) of flour. Knead the dough for 10 minutes. It should be smooth and slightly sticky. You may need more flour if it is too sticky. Place in a lightly oiled bowl. Dust with a little flour, cover and let rise for 30 minutes in a warm humid place.

Place the dough on a floured work surface and press it out to make a rectangle about 10 x 20 inches (25 x 51 cm) and about 1/2 inch (1.2 cm) thick. Brush the melted butter over the dough. Combine the Demerara and granulated sugars and cinnamon and sprinkle the mixture over the dough. Roll up jelly-roll fashion. Coat a sharp knife with flour to prevent sticking and cut the roll into 1 1/2-inch-thick (3.8-cm) slices. Place the slices on a greased baking sheet, allowing lots of room to expand. Leave 1 to 2 inches (2.5 to 5 cm) between each roll.

Cover and let rise for 30 minutes, or until doubled in size. Place in a preheated 375°F (190°C) oven for 15 to 20 minutes. Remove from the pan and cool on a rack. Sift the cocoa and icing sugar together, add the Kahlua and stir until smooth. Drizzle the mixture over the rolls. Start making the caffe latte.

Mango Yogurt Terrine

The sweet mango and the tart yogurt are a great combination. Serve it with a little whipped cream and slices of fresh mango.

1 Tbsp.	gelatin powder	15 mL
1 3/4 cups	whipping cream	420 mL
4 Tbsp.	icing sugar	60 mL
1 3/4 cups	mango yogurt	420 mL
2 tsp.	vanilla	10 mL

Soak the gelatin in 3 Tbsp. (45 mL) of the cream for 10 minutes.

Place the remaining cream and sugar in a saucepan and gently warm over medium heat. Whisk in the gelatin mixture and remove from the heat. Mix in the yogurt and vanilla. Strain. Pour into a 4-cup (1-L) mold and chill for 6 hours. Remove from the mold by dipping it into hot water for 30 seconds, then inverting it onto a plate. If it has melted too much, return it to the fridge for 30 minutes. Slice into portions with a hot knife.

DESSERTS

Pan-Fried Pineapples
with Cracked Pepper and Kahlua Sauce

During the days of the spice trade, real pepper was worth its weight in gold. To have fresh pineapples topped with cracked black pepper was truly a dish meant for kings and queens. We like to serve it with coconut ice cream.

FOR THE PINEAPPLE:

4	pineapple rings, about 5 inches (12.5 cm) across and 1 inch (2.5 cm) thick, peeled and cored	4
2 Tbsp.	cracked black pepper	30 mL
3 Tbsp.	butter	45 mL
1/4 cup	Kahlua or other coffee liqueur	60 mL

Sprinkle the pineapple with the pepper. Heat the butter in a frying pan over medium heat and add the pineapple. Pour in the Kahlua and ignite. Continue cooking for 2 minutes. Turn over and cook another 2 minutes. Remove from the heat and place on individual plates. Pour any extra sauce over the pineapple.

FOR THE SAUCE:

4 Tbsp.	butter	60 mL
1 cup	sugar	240 mL
1/2 cup	fresh orange juice	120 mL
3 Tbsp.	fresh lemon juice	45 mL
1/2 cup	Kahlua or other coffee liqueur	120 mL
1	orange, zest only	1

Heat the butter in a small saucepan over low heat until it browns. Set aside. In another pan, caramelize the sugar over medium heat until it's light golden brown. Stir in the orange and lemon juice and the Kahlua. Cook for 2 minutes. Stir in the butter and zest. Cool the sauce to room temperature.

TO ASSEMBLE:

4	scoops coconut ice cream	4
4 Tbsp.	icing sugar	60 mL

Top each pineapple slice with a scoop of ice cream and cover with the sauce. Garnish with pineapple leaves and icing sugar.

Pantry

Mayonnaise Base

Store-bought mayonnaise will last a long time, but once you start using fresh eggs to make your own, you must be extremely careful. Keep it in the refrigerator for no more than 3 to 4 days. Use this recipe as a base and add mustard, pepper, curry, garlic, dill or other herbs according to your personal taste.

1	large egg, slightly warmed	1
1 tsp.	rice wine vinegar	5 mL
	pinch salt	
1 1/3 cups	vegetable oil	320 mL

Crack the egg in a food processor and add the vinegar and salt. Process for 30 seconds. Add 1/4 cup (60 mL) of the oil and process 1 full minute. The slower you add the oil, the thicker the mayonnaise will be. Take your time. It should take about 3 minutes to incorporate all the oil. If it gets too thick you can add vinegar, water or lemon juice to thin it down.

Roasted Garlic Mayonnaise

This recipe goes well with French fries and makes a great dip for vegetables. You can also use it to glaze meat, fish or chicken.

1 recipe	Mayonnaise Base	1 recipe
1/3 cup	puréed roasted garlic (see page 13)	80 mL
1 Tbsp.	red wine vinegar	15 mL
	pinch salt and black pepper	
1 Tbsp.	sugar	15 mL

Place the mayonnaise in a bowl then add the roasted garlic, vinegar, salt, pepper and sugar. Mix well. Refrigerate until needed or store for up to 3 or 4 days.

PANTRY

Raspberry-Rosemary Vinagrette

This is a wonderful dressing for any salad and it complements goat cheese very well.

1/3 cup	raspberry vinegar	80 mL
1 Tbsp.	juice from pickled ginger	15 mL
1 tsp.	minced garlic	5 mL
1 Tbsp.	minced onion	15 mL
1 Tbsp.	chopped fresh chives	15 mL
1 Tbsp.	grenadine	15 mL
1 tsp.	minced lemon grass	5 mL
1 tsp.	salt	5 mL
1 tsp.	black pepper	5 mL
1/3 cup	rosemary oil	80 mL
1/3 cup	olive oil	80 mL

Mix the vinegar, pickled ginger juice, garlic, onion, chives, grenadine, lemon grass, salt and pepper in a measuring cup. In another cup, combine the oils. Pour 1/4 of the vinegar mixture into a mixing bowl and whisk in 1/4 of the oil, whisking until it's well combined. Repeat 3 more times. This dressing will keep for a week or so in the fridge. Whisk it well before each use.

Blackberry, Basil and Garlic Vinaigrette

This is excellent on salad greens, cooked or raw vegetables, or grilled fish.

1 cup	blackberries	240 mL
2 Tbsp.	minced onion	30 mL
2 Tbsp.	cider vinegar	30 mL
2 Tbsp.	red wine vinegar	30 mL
2 tsp.	minced garlic	10 mL
	pinch black pepper	
1 1/2 Tbsp.	sugar	22.5 mL
	pinch salt	
1 Tbsp.	chopped fresh basil	15 mL
1/3 cup	vegetable oil	80 mL
1/4 cup	olive oil	60 mL

Place the blackberries, onion, cider vinegar, red wine vinegar, garlic, black pepper, sugar, salt and basil in a large pot over medium heat. Simmer for 10 to 15 minutes, making sure the sugar is dissolved. Cool to room temperature and put the mixture into a blender. (Process in batches if necessary.) Purée the mixture, slowly adding the oils until it's emulsified.

Scallop Ravioli with Three-Cheese Alfredo
and Basil Pesto (page 122)

Night time view from the
Salmon House on the Hill

Rum-Soaked Salmon with
Apple Ginger Purée (page 107)

White and Dark Chocolate Mousse Pie
(page 158)
and Blood Orange Chiffon Cake
(page 164)

Chili Lime Aïoli

This is a great dipping sauce that goes well with just about anything. We put it on chicken satays and fried vegetable chips.

3	egg yolks	3
1 Tbsp.	minced garlic	15 mL
1/2 tsp.	black pepper	2.5 mL
1 Tbsp.	sambal oelek	15 mL
1/2 tsp.	salt	2.5 mL
1/2	lime, juice and zest	1/2
1 cup	vegetable oil	240 mL

Place the egg yolks, garlic, pepper and sambal oelek in a mixing bowl and whisk them together. Whisk in the salt, lime juice and zest. Slowly add the vegetable oil, whisking as you add it, until the mixture is thick. Because it is egg-based, this sauce will keep for only 3 days in the refrigerator.

Cumin Coconut Yogurt

We use this as a condiment with curry. The longer it sits, the thicker it gets.

2 cups	plain yogurt	475 mL
1 cup	toasted coconut	240 mL
1 tsp.	ground cumin	5 mL
	pinch salt and black pepper	

Mix everything together. It will keep for a week in the fridge, but after 2 to 3 days you will need to add more yogurt to keep it moist.

PANTRY

Hot and Sour Vinaigrette

East meets West in this useful condiment. Use it to dress vegetable salads, fish and shellfish, meat or chicken.

1	8-oz. (225-g) package fermented black beans	1
1 cup	ketchup	240 mL
1 cup	soy sauce	240 mL
2 Tbsp.	lemon juice	30 mL
1/4 cup	white vinegar	60 mL
1 Tbsp.	minced garlic	15 mL
1/2 tsp.	salt	2.5 mL
1 1/2 tsp.	black pepper	7.5 mL
1/4 cup	Demerara sugar	60 mL
1/4 cup	chopped green onion	60 mL
1/4 cup	minced sweet red pepper	60 mL
1/4 cup	minced sweet green pepper	60 mL
1 Tbsp.	sambal oelek	15 mL
1/4 cup	minced red onion	60 mL
1/2 cup	olive oil	120 mL

Put the black beans in a sieve and run under cold water for a couple of minutes until clean. Place all the ingredients in a large bowl and mix well. Cover and refrigerate until needed. It will keep a couple of weeks.

Apricot Chutney

Chutneys are traditional with curry, but we use this chutney in many other recipes.

3 Tbsp.	olive oil	45 mL
1/2 cup	minced onion	120 mL
1/2	minced lemon	1/2
1/2	minced lime	1/2
1/4 cup	minced sweet red pepper	60 mL
1/2 cup	raisins	120 mL
2 lb.	diced dried apricots	900 g
1 cup	Demerara sugar	240 mL
1 1/2 cups	malt vinegar	360 mL
1/2 cup	apple juice	120 mL
1/4 cup	white wine	60 mL

Heat the oil in a heavy saucepan over medium heat. Add the onion, lemon, lime, red peppers, raisins and apricots. Cook for about 10 minutes, until the onions are translucent. Add the sugar and cook for another minute, stirring constantly. Add the vinegar, juice and wine and simmer 1 to 1 1/2 hours, stirring occasionally to prevent sticking. The liquid should cook down so it's just below the level of the solids. Remove from the heat and cool before refrigerating. The chutney will keep in the fridge for at least a month.

ROASTING PEPPERS

To roast peppers, preheat the oven to 500°F (260°C). Put the peppers in a roasting pan and place in the oven, with the rack near the top. Roast, shaking the pan frequently, until the peppers shrivel and collapse, 30 to 40 minutes. Remove the peppers from the oven and place them in a bowl. Cover with plastic wrap. When they're cool, peel the peppers, discarding the skin, seeds and stem.

PANTRY

Tomato Curry Sauce

There are many types of curry sauce. This one goes particularly well with prawns and cauliflower.

2 Tbsp.	butter	30 mL
1/2 cup	minced onion	120 mL
2 tsp.	curry powder	10 mL
2 tsp.	turmeric	10 mL
1/2 tsp.	ground coriander	2.5 mL
1 tsp.	salt	5 mL
1 tsp.	black pepper	5 mL
1 tsp.	ground cumin	5 mL
1 tsp.	sambal oelek	5 mL
1 cup	vegetable stock (see page 58)	240 mL
2 cups	tomato juice	475 mL
1 cup	chopped ripe tomatoes, seeds and stems removed	240 mL
2 Tbsp.	honey	30 mL
2	chopped green onions	2

Melt the butter in a large frying pan over low heat. Add the onion, curry powder, turmeric, coriander, salt, pepper, cumin and sambal oelek. Sauté for 1 minute, until the mixture is lightly toasted.

Deglaze the pan with vegetable stock. Add the tomato juice, chopped tomato and honey. Simmer for 20 minutes.

Add the green onion and remove from the heat. This will keep in the fridge for up to 2 weeks.

Papaya Melon Lime Salsa

This is a standard sauce at the Salmon House. It's a great condiment for grilled fish or chicken.

1 cup	diced papaya	240 mL
1/4 cup	diced cantaloupe	60 mL
1/4 cup	diced sweet red pepper	60 mL
1/4 cup	diced red onion	60 mL
1/2 tsp.	black pepper	2.5 mL
	pinch salt	
1/2 tsp.	crushed dried chilies	2.5 mL
2 Tbsp.	lime juice	30 mL
2 Tbsp.	olive oil	30 mL

Mix everything together in a bowl and refrigerate until needed. It will keep for a week in the fridge.

Tomato Balsamic Salsa

Try this with nachos, tortillas or brochettes, or serve it chilled over grilled prawns, lobster and fish.

2 cups	chopped tomato, seeds and stem removed	475 mL
1/2 cup	diced red onion	120 mL
1/2 cup	chopped fresh basil	120 mL
1/2 tsp.	salt	2.5 mL
1/2 Tbsp.	black pepper	7.5 mL
1/2 Tbsp.	lemon juice	7.5 mL
1/2 cup	balsamic vinegar	120 mL
1/2 cup	olive oil	120 mL

Mix all the ingredients together and refrigerate. It will keep for a week in the fridge.

PANTRY

Tartar Sauce

Traditionally, a tartar sauce has been used as a dip for fish. But a sauce like this can be baked right on the fish or glazed on the fish after cooking.

1 cup	mayonnaise (see page 178)	240 mL
4 Tbsp.	minced dill pickle	60 mL
1 Tbsp.	pickle juice	15 mL
2 Tbsp.	chopped capers	30 mL
1 Tbsp.	caper juice	15 mL
1 Tbsp.	Dijon mustard	15 mL
1	lemon, juice and zest	1
1 Tbsp.	chopped fresh parsley	15 mL
1 Tbsp.	chopped fresh dill	15 mL
1	chopped green onion	1
1 tsp.	salt	5 mL
1 Tbsp.	lemon pepper	15 mL

Mix all the ingredients together in a bowl. Refrigerate. The sauce will keep for 3 days.

Cilantro Oil

Flavored oils not only add flavor to dishes but also give the plate some color.

1 cup	grapeseed oil	240 mL
1/4 cup	chopped cilantro	60 mL
1/2 tsp.	salt	2.5 mL

Place all ingredients in a blender and liquefy. It will last a month refrigerated, but if you plan to keep it that long, strain out the cilantro.

PANTRY

Index

INDEX